£5

THE GREATEST OF MY TIME

Trevor Bailey

THE GREATEST
OF MY TIME

Cartoons by Roy Ullyett

THE SPORTSMANS BOOK CLUB
London 1970

This Sportsmans Book Club edition was produced in 1970 for
sale to its members only by the proprietors, Readers Union
Limited, at Aldine House, 10-13 Bedford Street, London
W.C.2 and at Letchworth Garden City, Herts. Full details of
membership may be obtained from our London address.

Originally published by Eyre & Spottiswoode
Printed for Readers Union by Hollen Street Press Limited at
Slough

CONTENTS

PHOTOGRAPHS

Acknowledgements and thanks are due to the following for copyright photographs:

Central Press Photos Ltd for Nos 1–6, 8, 11–15, 17–24, 26, 28, 29, and 31–33; Keystone Press Agency Ltd for No 7; Sport and General Press Agency Ltd for Nos 9, 10, 25, 27, 34 and 35; P.A.–Reuter for No 16; and The Press Association Ltd for No 30.

PREFACE

Some time ago Gordon Ross invited me to write for the Playfair Cricket Monthly and I decided to do a series on the greatest players I had encountered. My aim was to analyse them as they appeared to me both as cricketers and as individuals. There was never any attempt to make an order of merit list and I simply wrote about those who possessed qualities which clearly placed them far above their fellows.

These portraits were well received, with the result that Eyre and Spottiswoode asked me to develop them into this book. The Playfair Cricket Monthly kindly agreed, and taking those pieces as a starting point I have considerably amended and extended them, and at the same time have added to their number. Now that this book has been completed I have one regret. Although all the cricketers included are there on merit, I have had to omit many who have almost equal claims – Hanif Mohammad, Wes Hall, Geoff Boycott, Neil Harvey, Frank Tyson, Lance Gibbs, Graeme Pollock and Neil Adcock to name but a few. Perhaps I shall be able in the future to write another collection.

One evening I ran into Roy Ullyett, whom I have known all my life, and I asked if I could reproduce some of his drawings. When I showed Roy what I was attempting he immediately volunteered to provide a cartoon in keeping with my text. Although Roy is generally considered to be the finest sporting cartoonist, whose drawings in the Daily Express add so much humour to the sports scene, I must confess I did not fully appreciate just how brilliant he is. In my opinion the cartoons he has drawn for this book are among the greatest he has done. Each in its way is a little classic and I would like to take this opportunity to thank him for his efforts which make me laugh every time I see them. I am certain that they will have a similar effect on readers.

T.E.B.

I

THE DON

The Greatest Batsman

I was brought up in the 1930s when Don Bradman was king and reigned supreme. To me, as a small boy, he was an idol and the greatest batsman the world had ever seen. My father might go into raptures over Jack Hobbs on a 'sticky' and the cover driving of Wally Hammond, but, ever a realist, I simply quoted the Don's unbeatable figures. Although he was one of the enemy, he made such an impression that I, in company with thousands of school-boys, always used the autographed Bradman bat in the vain hope that some of the magic might rub off on me. He literally bestrode the cricket scene. To me he will always remain the game's Napoleon, without a Waterloo even though his last Test innings was a duck, out second ball.

The Australians were a great team in those days, but a high percentage of the spectators came chiefly to see the small man with the big green cap and the insatiable appetite for runs. It was amazing how rarely he disappointed them. Nobody had ever approached his consistency. It is still difficult to believe that anyone can average 99 with the bat over a Test career which spanned some twenty years. I doubt whether we shall ever see his like again, for which bowlers everywhere will be more than thankful!

The Don was so much better in the vital task of amassing runs than all his contemporaries, yet in some respects this eventually proved to be almost a disservice to the game. Spectators would flock to the Australian grounds whenever the news reached them that the Don was batting, just as once many years before they had gone by hansom cab to see W. G. Grace at Lord's. Unfortunately, when the Don was eventually out, the followers dispersed. Such was his phenomenal drawing power that cricket

lost a large following when he retired, while several very promising young players were not exactly helped by being hailed as potential Bradmans. This is a ridiculous tag to put on any cricketer, however outstanding. The Don was unique, a young god, who played with mere mortals.

I was on the field when the Don played his last innings. The applause and the air of expectancy were unforgettable. He had been persuaded to take part in a one-day match against Sir Len Hutton's team and everyone hoped he would conjure up some of the magic which placed him so far above all other batsmen. Alas it was not to be as he soon chopped a ball from Brian Statham on to the stumps and departed back to the pavilion. Everything else was anti-climax. An era had ended. The emperor had passed away, never again to be seen in uniform.

I saw the Don in 1934 and in 1938. My hero did everything that was expected, amassed runs quickly and with almost clinical efficiency. Of course, the only series in which his batting was brought down to ordinary standards was when he faced Larwood and Voce in the notorious 'bodyline' tour, but even then he comfortably headed the Australian averages with 56·50.

It was not until 1948 that I played against him. He came to this country as captain of an exceptionally powerful Australian team who steam-rollered their way over England and the counties with the speed and efficiency of a German Blitzkrieg. I bowled against him then on three occasions, for Essex, for Gentlemen of England, and in the Hastings Festival. He was past his prime, but he scored 187, 150 and 143 and supplied me with three very good reasons for placing him as the finest batsman I have ever bowled against. I did have the satisfaction of claiming his wicket on one occasion – but it was only with a long hop after he had decided he had plundered sufficiently!

Why did he score so many runs? There were five main reasons : the first was the inevitability in the way he dealt with the bad ball. He did not merely hit the loose delivery and hope it was going to the boundary, he despatched it there. A particularly fine example of this occurred in the Essex massacre at Southend, when the Australians made 721 runs in the day. The Essex captain,

Tom Pearce, decided to put on our second leg-spinner, Frank Vigar, for a psychological first over immediately preceding the luncheon interval. The result was catastrophic, as Don helped himself to six consecutive fours. I was originally stationed at mid-on, but, though I finished at deep mid-wicket the result was exactly the same, another boundary. All six were perfectly executed, along the ground and obvious fours before they had even left his bat.

Secondly, the Don saw the ball earlier than most people and this, combined with his exceptional reflexes and footwork, meant that he was in a position to play shots that nobody else attempted. Don himself provided me with one of the most revealing examples of this when for once, after a fine dinner, I managed to induce him to talk about his own batting, something which he does rarely. He recalled a match in Australia when a fast-medium seamer called Ginty Lush was bowling at him with the wicket-keeper standing up. The Don suggested that in the interests of safety it would be wiser for him to stand back as he intended to flick one backwards and a nasty accident could occur. Normally, he did not indulge in such batting flippancies, but the fact that he could contemplate, and execute, such a strike against an accomplished bowler in a first-class game underlined his genius. Also, as a young man he could cross-bat a short ball from a really fast bowler along the ground between mid-wicket and mid-on. In other words he was able to *pull* them early from outside the line, or in front of his face, rather than getting inside the line to *hook*. He was so very quick on his feet that he was probably the most difficult batsman to contain there has been; indeed the speed of his footwork enabled him to hit many balls to the boundary on the full toss which a normal cricketer would have had to play from the crease. When confronted with the problem of body-line which was both physically dangerous and tactically successful, he attempted to solve the dual threat by stepping to leg and cutting some of the short deliveries into the vacant areas on the off side. When one considers the exceptional pace of Harold Larwood and Bill Voce, one realizes just how quickly Don had to move his feet to be in a position to execute such a shot.

Thirdly, Bradman possessed superb powers of concentration and regarded a century as a springboard for bigger things.

Fourthly, he possessed a fine defence. Nobody can make as many runs as he did without being basically sound. He certainly lifted his bat to third man, which helped when playing cross-bat shots off the back foot, but nobody brought it down straighter, when playing defensively back as well as forward – that, after all, is the vital thing.

Finally, Bradman believed in reducing the number of chances of losing his wicket to a minimum and so generally kept the ball along the carpet. A six may be an exciting shot, but if the timing is not perfect a catch can easily result.

One interesting facet of his batting was the way he so often scored faster than he appeared to be doing. In one match to my amazement the scoreboard announced his 50, while I was convinced he was no further than the early 20s. I still marvel at the 300 he made in one day of the Test match in Leeds in 1934. Admittedly the game was not 'closed up' so much in those days, but it remains a wondrous feat of batsmanship.

Although his skill with the bat overshadows all else, he was in his youth one of the greatest outfields that Australia has produced. He was fast, picked up the ball beautifully on the run, never seemed to drop a catch, and possessed a strong flat accurate return which was a source of constant delight to spectators. His throwing action was very high and brought him a goodly number of victims run out.

As a captain, the Don was shrewd and tough. In 1948 he was fortunate in having an exceptionally powerful team under his command, but there is no denying that he capitalized on his assets to the utmost. He always held the view that it did not matter who captured the wickets, the important thing was to remove the opposition quickly. On that particular tour Toshack did not claim all that number of victims, yet he became an integral part of the Aussie attack and provided the pacemen – Lindwall, Miller and Johnston – with a breathing space before another assault with the new ball. As a tactician he has had few equals. As a leader, he was by nature rather aloof and self-

15

sufficient, and he was respected by rather than popular with his team. Perhaps he had difficulty in understanding those whose personalities were essentially far removed from his own. He was definitely not a romantic in outlook.

Underneath the Don's somewhat reserved exterior lurks a distinct, if somewhat sardonic, sense of humour and an agile wit. This was typified in the remark he made to Walter Robins, a great personal friend, when he came into our dressing room after play in Gentlemen of England v. The Australians at Lord's in 1948. At that time there were many who felt that the lively Middlesex captain was the ideal person to revitalize the national team. In the course of the game, Ray Lindwall unleashed a lethal, playful bouncer which nearly decapitated Robins and left him sitting on the ground. In addition to certain physical similarities, the Don and Robbie were kindred souls. Certainly nobody appreciated Don's dry comment more, when he said, 'It's a good thing you didn't try to make a comeback, Robbie : we'd have dropped you !'

I did not, of course, know Bradman in his early years when a rather ruthless outlook, combined with a fierce ambition to succeed and a dedicated approach, inevitably made him something of a 'loner', with remarkable self-sufficiency, far removed from the typical Australian. Now age, success and the influence of a particularly charming wife (who is an outstanding hostess) have mellowed him.

He is a very interesting character, a shrewd business man and a lover of classical music. He is also exceptionally talented as an after-dinner speaker, which is something of a rarity in Australia.

The Don was a natural games player and I believe that he could have been either a great tennis or a golf champion if he had concentrated on these sports, indeed with his approach and co-ordination of eye and muscle he was bound to be well above average at any game. In addition to his natural ability he possesses a very agile brain and I have always found him fascinating on cricket, once he can be persuaded to talk. Unlike so many of the great players who, when they retire, have difficulty in appreciating the technical changes and are forever looking backwards, he is able to appreciate and understand the good and the bad developments. He realizes that 'scientific' field placing has made the scoring of runs quickly much more difficult, while bowlers are more prepared to contain than they were when he was at his peak. At times he must be frustrated by some of the less attractive trends, but he is still able to keep his sense of proportion and his toleration. In these circumstances it is easy to understand why he is an excellent writer on the game – his match accounts are among the best I have read, factual and fair.

When he retired Don Bradman became an administrator and today is the most important man in this department of Australian cricket. I was particularly impressed by the way the authorities there tackled the problem of throwing. They may have been ruthless, but they certainly eliminated all the suspects very quickly. In England there is a tendency to set up an investigating committee whenever a difficulty arises. It may be democratic, but it is sometimes unnecessary and nearly always means delay.

I would not rate Don as the batsman I would most like to watch, for he appeared too machine-like; but of all batsmen he is the one I would most like to have on my side.

2

LEN HUTTON

The Master

The two finest English batsmen who played before and after the war were Sir Leonard Hutton and Denis Compton. They towered above their contemporaries but were entirely dissimilar in character, outlook and technique. Hutton was the more complete craftsman and seldom matched, or attempted to match Compton's inspired improvisation. Batting to Len was essentially a business – and a highly profitable one. To Denis it always remained something of a game.

Few cricketers have been more dedicated to the job of making runs than Len. In an Essex match against Yorkshire Len was not out overnight having scored a fine century. When I arrived at the ground on the following day, Len was practising in the nets. Apparently he was not entirely happy about his cover drive though I had seen nothing wrong with it. In addition to his keenness to practise was a fierce determination to succeed and exceptional powers of concentration, which were never more clearly shown than in his world record score of 364 against the Australians in 1938 at The Oval.

Surely it must have been a Yorkshireman who first said 'Look after the pennies and the pounds will take care of themselves'? Not that the 'tyke' is ungenerous, quite the reverse, but he is careful: money has to be earned and therefore it ought never to be squandered rashly. Len brought to the problem of acquiring money all the thought, tenacity and concentration which epitomized his batting, and it was hardly surprising that he should be a success in the commercial world. It was almost inevitable. He was certainly the only first-class cricketer I knew who read the stocks and shares before the sports page.

This attitude is typified in Yorkshiremen's cricket. Their

batsmen are brought up to make runs by sound, rather than by spectacular methods, because this is more likely to produce results over a period of time. Their bowlers are instructed to be tight misers who do not believe in making presents of half-volleys and full tosses. It is characteristic that the Yorkshire side has never permanently carried that most expensive of bowlers, the wrist-spinner. They have preferred to rely on the more accurate finger-spinner even if he is liable to take longer to achieve results on a good wicket. As Len Hutton once said to Peter May after he had lost his wicket to a somewhat flamboyant stroke in the West Indies, 'You don't play cricket for fun, Peter, you know'.

The essential difference between the batting technique of Len Hutton and Denis Compton was that Len had a pronounced initial forward movement, while Denis, certainly to quick bowling, moved back and across. Both methods have a certain advantage and disadvantage, although the majority of great players, especially from overseas, favour the latter method.

The forward mover is earlier in position to deal effectively with the slightly over-pitched delivery and it followed that Len was a superb driver. On the other hand, an initial forward movement is liable to prove a handicap when facing fast short bowling, because it takes longer and requires more movement to be able to make a hook and Denis, as a result, played this shot much better. Nevertheless, Len was a firm advocate of playing forward to the new ball, or at least half-cock with the weight on the front foot. There is much in favour of this technique in England, where the ball is more liable to move off the seam. Once on the back foot there is always a good chance of being lbw to the ball that nips back off the pitch. Personally, I always fancied bowling to a back player whenever it was possible to achieve movement off the pitch, but it was a different matter overseas on a plumb pitch.

One of the chief reasons I found myself pressed into opening the batting for England was because of Len's belief in the value of forward play against the new ball. Conversely this is probably also why Reg Simpson, a glorious player of pace bowling off the back foot, did not have as many opportunities in international cricket as his ability warranted.

354

Sir Leonard

The first time I was asked to open the innings with Hutton was in a Test Trial at Edgbaston in 1953. I was only told about this decision some fifteen minutes before the commencement of play, so I changed surreptitiously, mentioned the matter to nobody and at the psychological moment appeared ready for the fray before my understandably startled colleagues. Reg Simpson, who was down on the scorecard as number two, was especially baffled. In the following winter Len decided to continue the experiment against the West Indies as the M.C.C. opening stands in the early matches had not been over-productive, while I had sometimes run out of partners from my established position in the middle of the order. (In the first Test at Sabina Park things reached such a state that almost unbelievably my first scoring stroke was a six! Four wickets had tumbled, while I was meditating, surveying the bowlers, and generally acclimatizing myself. Suddenly, I realized Alan Moss was coming down the pavilion steps. Even Alan's closest friends did not consider him the most dependable of batsmen, and the time had clearly come for desperate measures!)

I went in first with Len in both the fourth and the fifth Tests. It did not provide the runs that I would have liked, although we managed to put on 73 on the mat in Trinidad, and in Jamaica, when I had the rare experience of opening both the bowling and the batting on the same day, we put on 44. I was once again resurrected as an opener in Australia in 1954–5. Len seemed to think I made an ideal sacrificial lamb. His theory was that, as Lindwall and Miller were liable to remove anyone with the new ball, it might just as well be me. At least this allowed me to register my most distinguished duck! I struggled for forty-five minutes without being able to edge even a single and was eventually dismissed with my score sheet still virgin, but at least the opening bowlers had come off.

There were a number of advantages about going in first for England with Len. It is always a pleasure to be closely associated with real class even when it underlines one's own deficiencies the more clearly. He made batting appear so simple and, as a distinctly utilitarian performer I found his judgement of a run especially helpful. Although he was no sprinter between the wickets, he never missed a single and one had the comforting knowledge that there was little chance of being run out. Len also knew when not to run. At Sabina Park the West Indies attempted to blast their way back into the game through their fast bowler, King. At the other end Gomez operated at around military medium. While I weaved and ducked the King bumpers, which often averaged four per over, Len chuckled as he dealt elegantly with Gomez. Nobody appreciated the joke more, especially when King was eventually forced to retire with a muscle injury, a direct outcome of his surfeit of bouncers.

The forward mover, against slow bowling on a pitch receptive to spin, has an advantage when the ball leaves the bat, but he has more difficulty with the delivery that comes in to him. Naturally, both Len Hutton and Denis Compton were real artists on a 'sticky' or 'crumbler', but if Jim Laker and Tony Lock were to be operating against them under these conditions I would fancy Jim to have more chance of dismissing Len, but the reverse would apply to Tony. If a player as great as Len can be said to have possessed a weakness, it was probably against off-spin and in-swing bowling. It is remarkable how many times Ian Johnson, not an especially great off-break bowler, claimed his wicket in Test cricket, while Worcester's Reg Perks, who made the new ball dip in sharply, had his moments against him.

One of my great regrets is that during the Brisbane Test in 1950–1 Len batted down the order so that we did not see enough of him on a notorious Australian 'sticky'. The theory behind this decision was that our middle order was brittle, but it turned out to be a waste of talent. (Although this was by no means as odd as including Arthur Macintyre, the second wicket-keeper, as a batsman and a possible bowler, merely because he had turned his arm over adequately in the *nets*!) I was lucky enough to bat with Hutton for some fifteen minutes before our declaration and it was remarkable how seldom he appeared to be in trouble, despite a pitch which many people deemed impossible, and on which Australia had lost seven wickets for under forty runs. He played superbly in our second innings and throughout that tour he looked a class higher than any batsman on either side.

Perhaps the most fascinating feature of Len's batting was its technical perfection. He remained interesting to watch even when he was scoring slowly! Not that this occurred often because he was such a master of his craft that he would keep the score ticking over by merely placing the ball. This was one of the main problems I found when bowling against him. On occasions, I would feel that I was not doing too badly, until a glance at the scoreboard reminded me that Len's total had steadily mounted without my being really aware of the fact. He would take a single here, angle one down to third man, and tuck the ball neatly off his legs for two, while always at the back of the bowler's mind was the knowledge that a bad delivery would be despatched to the boundary. There was a professional certainty about his batting that made a big innings appear not only probable but almost inevitable once he was set. I used to hope I might have him caught round the corner early on with one that came back off the pitch, or possibly at slip from a lifter. Unfortunately, these dismissals occurred rather more frequently in my dreams than in reality.

On rare occasions, Len would abandon his correct, orthodox approach and cut loose with a flurry of strokes that left everyone breathless. In Australia they still speak of his innings in the second Test match at Sydney in 1947. He only scored 37, but it was out of 49 and lasted a mere 24 minutes. This was against Lindwall and Miller in full cry and contained some of the most brilliant stroke play ever seen on that ground. On the following tour in our second innings at Brisbane, only shortage of partners prevented him scoring what would surely have been one of the most scintillating and artistic centuries ever played there. However, these were merely moments of magic in the career of a batsman who made the majority of his runs by sound, beautifully produced strokes, enlivened by the best cover drive since Wally Hammond's. Having seen him play so many epic innings, it is not easy to single out one in particular, but his two-day innings of 205 at Sabina Park in the fifth Test against the West Indies in 1954 must have been one of his finest. During this marathon I only saw him make one false stroke! He never looked as if there was any danger of his losing his wicket and he simply went on and on methodically acquiring runs.

Len Hutton became captain of England because he was the finest batsman in the country, an established Test player, possessed a very wide knowledge of the game, and was strongly supported by the popular press, but his appointment was only grudgingly received by many of the game's hierarchy who failed to appreciate the social revolution that was taking place. Thus Len was the first professional to captain England. With a blare of publicity and with relatively little experience of captaincy he was given the job of leading the M.C.C. in the West Indies. Because of the rather delicate political situation which then existed in the Caribbean and because the series was for the unofficial championship of the world, it was almost certainly bound to be a controversial tour. Unfortunately this was not appreciated by those responsible for selecting the side to make the trip and, whereas two managers and sometimes more were considered necessary for Australia, it was felt that a player-manager, C. H. Palmer, with little overseas experience, plus a very inexperienced captain would be sufficient. Len was determined to prove a success in his new role. He never spared himself and it took a great deal out of his far from robust frame, both mentally and physically. He had never found it easy to relax and the increased responsibilities made it even more difficult, so that he often became and looked very tired. There is bound to be a certain amount of strain in leading England and this, combined with his efforts to retain his position as the leading opening batsman in the world, caused his retirement from the game earlier than might otherwise have happened. Even so, I sometimes feel that, if Yorkshire had followed England's example and made him their captain, he might have been tempted to carry on longer. He certainly would have found it hard to refuse.

He had served a tough apprenticeship with the pre-war Yorkshire XI, when his county was the most important single factor in English cricket. He had been raised to play hard, to give 'nowt', and to expect 'nowt' in return. He only gambled on certainties. He brought this practical and rather uncompromising approach to his captaincy. He proved exceptionally successful as the England skipper, rather than popular. He was, perhaps, a shade too remote from his own team and had little time for the opposition. On the field he fought his Test campaigns hard and efficiently, while off it there was comparatively little fraternization.

His assessment of the weaknesses of opposing batsmen was masterly and he regarded any looseness on the part of his bowlers as criminal. His tactics were thoroughly Yorkshire in their conception and eminently sound in their execution, a blend of attack and defence. He believed in attacking a batsman up until the moment that it looked as if this policy might cost runs. When this occurred he would try to shut him up and make him work for them. From his own batsmen he expected runs. He had sympathy when they lost their wicket, providing they had not contributed to their own downfall through a rash or ill-judged stroke.

Personally, I enjoyed playing under Len as in many respects our outlook was similar and during our long association I cannot recall any disagreement. However, some cricketers found him hard to fathom, while he himself had some difficulty in appreciating the more liberal approach, of, say, Denis Compton.

Because of his own mastery and preference for slow bowling, on occasions he put too much faith in speed. Two examples of this occurred in the first Test against the West Indies in 1953–4 and against Australia at Brisbane in 1954–5. In both these matches he took the field with top heavy attacks which relied on four fast bowlers. Because the vital principle of balance was neglected we twice crashed to heavy defeat. However, his handling of his attack was very good and often inspired, while his field placing was excellent. He realized that to seek advice from time to time was a sign of strength and not of weakness and this paid dividends. The only occasion I can remember him making a serious tactical blunder was at Leeds against the Australians in 1953, when he misread the venom in the pitch and the situation. As a result of a somewhat laboured rearguard action England avoided what at one time seemed probable defeat. Eventually, when our second innings closed Australia needed 177 in an hour and fifty-two minutes. In normal circumstances this was hardly obtainable but Len, remembering the way they had collapsed against Wardle at Manchester, decided to go for a win. He opened with Lock and Bedser plus ultra attacking fields. Runs came so fast that before Len knew what was happening, he had surrendered the initiative and victory was within our opponents' grasp. This was avoided by a spell of negative leg side bowling on my part which should never have been required.

Len has always been a quiet, sensitive and rather solitary individual. He is seldom to be found in a crowd, he is a natural introvert who prefers to brood alone. The cares of the England captaincy made him retreat still further into himself so that it became even more difficult to come close to him. He seemed sometimes to be suspicious of friendship, as though it stemmed from an ulterior motive.

I remember him one evening in Australia when he was feeling the strain of captaining England at the same time as maintaining his own very high standards of batsmanship. He told me he was worried because people in general, and the press in particular, tended to regard anything less than a century from him as tantamount to failure. In the end it seemed he no longer enjoyed the act of accumulating runs. The only satisfaction he obtained was after the event.

Some players were of the impression that Hutton lacked a sense of humour, but they were wrong. Possibly they were unable to appreciate his particular brand of wit, for it was essentially dry and quiet. He had a habit of sidling up to one in the dressing-room and, *sotto voce*, making a remark usually sardonic. He then would slip away, chuckling silently to himself as he did so.

3

CYRIL WASHBROOK

The Complete Professional

It has always been a great advantage for a cricket team to possess a reliable opening pair of batsmen and there is no doubt that England's finest since the war was Hutton and Washbrook. Both had been reared on the best pre-war traditions of the two most powerful northern counties and the influence of their rather stern, and fiercely competitive upbringing was clearly reflected in their batting. They were completely professional in their approach to the job of making runs and providing the foundation for a large total. To them this was a serious business in which flippancy was entirely out of place. The traditional rivalry between the White and the Red Rose added the spice of personal and traditional competition, although this never interfered with the task in hand. Above all they were both complete craftsmen and therefore automatically respected and appreciated these qualities in each other. It followed that they ran very well between the wickets because they had faith in each other's judgement.

Although Hutton and Washbrook had the same practical northern outlook, effective rather than scintillating, their individual styles and techniques were entirely different. Len was taller and his strokes rather more flowing. Cyril sported a cap, which he wore at a distinctly rakish angle, almost as a protest against convention, and looked more pugnacious. The Lancastrian relied far more on cross bat shots for his runs and was always on the look out for the short delivery to cut or hook. Cyril played both these strokes extremely well, and, though they sometimes caused his downfall they also brought him a vast number of runs. Despite his reputation as a hooker, however, I was far more impressed by the power and precision of his square cutting. Anything just short of a length outside the off stump he would send scudding

Enter CYRIL
— and long
leg was alerted
for one down
his throat

to the boundary, leaning into the ball, bringing the bat down and rolling his wrists in order to make sure that it was played along the carpet.

Whenever Essex played Lancashire, we automatically stationed our fine leg somewhat squarer in the hope that Cyril would hole out there from the hook. We trapped him in this way on the odd occasion, but in between he made us pay dearly, because, although he usually hooked up, he also played this stroke most proficiently.

Cyril was a batsman of true international calibre from which it followed that he possessed an excellent defence, watching each delivery right on to the face of the bat, and was technically sound. He was an ideal opener, equally at home against pace or spin, imperturbable, hard, and able to adjust the tempo of his run rate to the situation. Although not an outstanding driver, he naturally could play this shot when he so desired, while his cover slash-cum-drive off his front foot was both effective and exciting. However, he was a master at tucking the ball away off his legs and keeping the score moving along by means of the well placed single. He was particularly good on a bad wicket when, in addition to his sound defence, he had the ability to improvise brilliantly.

Apart from Hutton, Compton and Graveney, I would rate him the best player I have seen since the war on a really difficult pitch.

When I first encountered Cyril, I was naturally impressed not only by his reputation but by the obvious quality of his batting and fielding. My respect increased when, together with Winston Place, he took 120 runs in forty-five minutes off the Essex new ball attack chasing a total against the clock, but as a person he seemed rather aloof, somewhat supercilious, and distinctly unapproachable.

Later, when I played Test cricket and toured Australia with him, I discovered yet again that the real person and the outward appearance were very different. Basically shy, Cyril became an altogether different character once you knew him. He was a most engaging companion, extremely interesting on a number of subjects, and a shrewd practical business man. Under the surface there was also that well-developed sense of humour which I have grown to expect from a Lancastrian.

29

His knowledge of cricket was extensive and listening to his views made me appreciate even more the value of discussing the game with a real expert. Before the war, county cricketers spent far more time on this than they do today, and they were unquestionably the better for it. I found Cyril's advice excellent, but it seemed to me that he was sometimes chary of giving it in case it was not received with the interest which it certainly deserved.

In addition to being England's opening batsman, Cyril Washbrook was the most accomplished player that Lancashire has produced for a very long time. As senior professional, and later as captain, and a member of the county committee, he exerted a considerable influence on his county's affairs. I once played under Cyril on tour, when both Freddie Brown and Denis Compton did not perform and I was impressed by the way he handled the side. On this occasion he was, however, unlucky in losing a pre-match tactical battle with the opposing skipper. Cyril won the toss and would naturally have batted, on what was one of the most perfect tracks I have encountered, but his opposite number persuaded him that it would be in the best interests of gate receipts if they had first strike and he acquiesced. It was only a two-day affair and we were not very happy when the locals proceeded to occupy the crease for the entire day. In desperation our slow bowlers endeavoured to give them runs, but they merely meandered contentedly along at around twenty-five runs per hour. We became even more incensed when they continued to bat on the following day and despite our lack of true pace, even hurled down some bouncers and beamers to enliven the proceedings. Their long delayed declaration came at lunchtime, at which moment the heavens opened up and we never had an opportunity to bat at all. After that experience Cyril must have viewed the prospect of putting the opposition in with even greater suspicion.

As a captain Cyril was tactically sound and, inevitably, perhaps, leaned towards caution rather than high adventure. His inclination was always towards setting an extremely difficult target, probably working on the principle that it is always easy to give runs away once the enemy has dropped behind the clock and started to lose interest than to shut this down when it is in full pursuit. However, he was never a real believer in this brand of charity. He preferred to win on merit, rather than try opening the game up by declaration and counter-declaration.

His appraisals of the strength and weaknesses of opponents were shrewd in the extreme. He would have made a good captain for England, or any powerful side. Why then was he not more successful for Lancashire, first as skipper and later as manager?

There were three main reasons, it seems to me. First, he never commanded a team that had sufficient balance necessary to secure the County Championship without a great deal of luck and therefore he was never able to produce the results which his county demanded. Lancashire, with their fine cricketing tradition, feel that it is their right to be near the top of the table. Secondly, his seniority, ability and personality all conspired to make him appear somewhat remote and even austere. Thirdly, he had a tendency to demand rather too high a standard from his players, especially the bowlers. Possibly he was spoilt by having Brian Statham in his side – a person who has always rated one bad ball per day a needless extravagance. Cyril gave the impression that he expected the rest of his attack to measure up to the same degree of excellence. I always felt, for instance, that he never fully appreciated the worth of Roy Tattersall, who was a very fine bowler with exceptional control, but never spun the ball sufficiently to become another Laker. Lancashire were to dispose of Roy's services eventually while he was still one of the finest slow bowlers in the country and without a comparable replacement, a decision that cost them many matches. This habit of expecting too much from bowlers is a very common failing with county captains who have spent a long time in the higher strata of cricket. I have lost count of the number of times that one of them has come up to me after Essex have scraped together a reasonable total on an indifferent pitch, and said, quite correctly, 'You wouldn't have made fifty against Laker and Lock on that wicket'. He has then proceeded to blame his bowlers for failing to exploit the helpful conditions. In other words skippers are inclined to want the same quality from county bowlers as from two outstanding internationals. This may well be desirable, but it simply is not practical. One must always be prepared to make the most of what one has at one's disposal.

In one respect Cyril was fortunate, that when he was elected captain of Lancashire he was given considerably more latitude and freedom from interference than many of his predecessors. He did not, for example, have to put up with the problem of receiving a telegram at the commencement of play from a distinguished member of the committee giving instructions as to who should open the bowling.

One of the more interesting changes that has taken place in cricket since the war has been the gradual decrease in importance of the position of cover point. This has been largely due to increase of off-spin, in-swing, and short-of-a-length bowling, which has restricted the number of off-side scoring strokes. In Cyril Washbrook's early days cover was regarded as a key specialist position, in the same way as the 'bat-pad' station and the short leg is today. Even now when a really fast bowler is operating he will often only have one fieldsman in front of the bat on the off side and it is then vital that the fieldsman should be like the old time cover, fast and nimble, but he is really a short extra, rather than a genuine cover point. When a good off-break or in-swing bowler is bowling the job of cover can safely be entrusted to one of the less outstanding fieldsmen. Nevertheless, a class cover, like Colin Bland, is still a considerable asset. He should be quick off the mark, have the ability to pick up quickly and neatly, and possess a fast accurate throw. Personally, I have always believed that he should vary his position from time to time and try to lure the batsman into a false sense of security by making him think that there is a short single to be had. He should also be able to hit the stumps direct, with some degree of consistency, especially at the bowler's end. His job is to prevent boundaries and at the same time to make the pinching of sharp singles an unprofitable business. Cyril Washbrook, until the arrival of Robin Hobbs, was the last England cricketer to be regarded as a specialist cover-point and he was very good at his job. He patrolled his domain with an imperial swagger, his cap, as always, at a rakish angle over one eye. The batsman who imagined there was a run to be had in his area frequently learned his lesson the hard way.

4

W. J. EDRICH

The Fighter

The County Championship is normally won by a well-balanced team with a powerful attack, but when Middlesex carried off the title in 1947 it was largely because of the exceptional quality and strength of their batting.

Bowling against Middlesex was more of a problem then than bowling against many Test teams. Not only did they score heavily, but they aimed, and frequently succeeded in having over 400 runs on the board by tea on the first day. They had a formidable opening pair in the elegant Jack Robertson, who made over 2,700 runs, and the efficient Sid Brown who also topped the 2,000 mark. Then came Bill Edrich and Denis Compton. In that golden summer this pair amassed between them 7,355 runs, a feat which will surely stand forever. It was runs and roses all the way for both of them and I used to think that the best chance of removing either was for one to run the other out.

But how did these two compare as players? Denis was a genius. Bill was a great player, who in his prime would have been an automatic selection for a world eleven.

Bill was a complete batsman with a magnificent defence (few in my experience have watched the ball more closely) and a wide range of attacking strokes. All the outstanding small players have hooked and pulled well, because they are in a position for these strokes a shade quicker than bigger men. Bill was no exception. He was a superb and fearless hooker of the fastest bowling. To see him hook Ray Lindwall was one of the most exhilarating sights that the game has produced.

Again in company with most small, nimble batsmen, Bill was very quick on his feet against the spinners and his cutting was of the highest order. He also perfected a lofted stroke wide of mid on, a pulled drive which was a cross between the on drive and the 'cow shot', which brought him a vast number of sixes on even the largest of grounds. What used to surprise me was how such a short person could hit the ball so high and so far, but of course his timing was exceptional.

As the years went by, Bill lost some of his freedom, and although because of his quite magnificent defensive technique, he was never easy to dismiss, it became possible to keep him relatively quiet by bowling a full length on and just outside the off stump, something which would never have occurred in 1947.

When Bill eventually retired from first-class cricket he returned to his native Norfolk. Understandably he had had his fill of cricket six days per week and found that it was beginning to pall. Moreover Minor County Cricket is very different. The standard is not so high – the second XI of a first-class county is often considerably stronger than a Minor county – it is less professional in both outlook and application, and with only two-day matches and a limited programme is not nearly so exacting or demanding. Bill found the new ingredients very much to his liking and it gave his cricket career a new lease of life. He enjoyed it rather more than his last few years with Middlesex and rendered Norfolk great service as captain and as player. His experience and his knowledge were of enormous value, just in fact what a Minor county needed.

Bill is of course the most distinguished member of the greatest cricketing family of this generation : Brian played for Kent, Geoff for Lancashire, and his nephew John for Surrey and England. Every year the Edrich clan assemble to take part in a charity match (as an Edrich XI), tough yeomen stock who clearly relish a battle.

Bill was a born fighter. This was the most outstanding feature of his batting, and indeed of his life. The bowling could be fast and the ball lifting off a length, but you could guarantee that Bill would be right behind every delivery. He was prepared to accept the hardest knocks without flinching, indeed they only served to increase his determination. His pugnacious chin would simply be thrust out a shade further and he would fight on. On one occasion I was batting with him and he received a very painful knock. I asked him how he was and, without bothering to rub

35

3,539.

BATTLING BILL
In War and Peace!

Roy ULLYETT.

the bruised spot, he replied in typical Edrich fashion, 'Of course I'm all right, let's get on with the game'. Another time in the nets at Perth, which were hard and very fast, a delivery from Frank Tyson rose sharply and just flicked the end of his nose. To my surprise he just shook his head and carried on as if this was merely an everyday occurrence. He certainly inspired confidence in his partners and was always willing to help by taking more than his share of the bowling when they were in difficulties, or trying to settle down. I would like him on my side at any time, but especially when the going was rough. He was just the type of player England needed in 1963 to combat the physical dangers provided by Wes Hall and Charlie Griffith.

It is hardly surprising that Bill should have had a distinguished war career. He learned to fly and became a bomber pilot in a squadron that specialized in daylight raids. Perhaps because I am romantic at heart and lived through those turbulent days, I have a passionate admiration for those who flew with the RAF during the war. To me they will always represent the best that this country has produced.

Bill joined Middlesex as a professional in the mid-1930s and was soon recognized as one of the most promising young players in the country at a time when there was no shortage. Playing at Lord's undoubtedly helped, but there was no disguising his class and he went on two overseas tours before the war. He had an indifferent series against Australia in England in 1938 and in South Africa he was unable to find his best form until the final timeless Test match when he justified his captain, Wally Hammond's faith with an innings of 219 not out. When the war came, Bill was established as an international player who was approaching his zenith.

At the end of hostilities Bill, with a D.F.C. to his credit, returned to Middlesex, but after one season he decided to become an amateur. It was still considered essential to have an amateur captaining England and at that time it seemed probable that Bill, who was an automatic choice as a player, would assume command when Hammond retired. Before the war, Hammond had taken the similar step of turning amateur and had been rewarded with the leadership of his county. Bill never achieved this distinction for a number of reasons which included a marked disregard for the hierarchy at Lord's – almost tantamount to heresy at the time – an unconventional outlook, a certain wildness of spirit and an impetuosity which would have been worshipped in Dublin, and a refusal to conform to standards laid down by others. However, his decision to turn amateur undoubtedly cost him at least £10,000 of untaxed income, which is what he would have received if he had remained a professional and taken the Benefit to which he was entitled. Of course at that particular time nobody envisaged Benefits producing sums of this nature, while the captaincy of England, besides the honour and glory also had considerable commercial value.

Bill Edrich lived and played hard. He believed that life was for living, not for existing. Now was the vital time and he was never unduly concerned about the morrow, an attitude which his experiences as a combat pilot had probably helped to develop. I always felt that he needed at least a thirty-six hour day and a trip by car with him at the wheel was not for the nervous. He had exceptional stamina and a remarkable constitution. He was not the type of cricketer who thought it necessary, or desirable, to retire early just because there happened to be a Test match on the following day. Fiercely independent, and sometimes headstrong, Bill went his own way expecting to be judged only by his performances on the field which were normally outstanding. Inevitably, though, there were those in authority who were out of sympathy with this outlook. I remember how he upset one rather precise and sedate selector, who unfortunately had an adjoining room, by retiring to bed at an hour when the milkman had already been out and about for some time. The ethical gulf which divided these two men was enormous. The selector, a former England captain, was utterly devoted and dedicated to cricket, regarding it with something close to reverence, but to Bill it always remained a game, which he had no intention of allowing to interfere with his private life. On that following morning, a Monday, Bill, who was not out, proceeded to make seventy-odd runs in fine style.

In 1950–1 England went to Australia under Freddie Brown and left Bill behind. This was a crass error which may well have cost us the Ashes. The captain and the selectors decided to gamble on a number of inexperienced and unproven batsmen, who would cause no problems or difficulties, but lacked class and could not conceivably be expected to produce as many runs as Bill. We lost the first and the second Tests simply because we were short of one outstanding batsman. Both were close, tense matches – just the type to have brought out the very best in Bill – and a couple of fifties, which were certainly well within his scope, could have turned the scales in our favour even though we were not as strong as the Australians. In retrospect it is interesting to note that when Len Hutton, whose main consideration was always to defeat the enemy, became captain, Bill was recalled to the international scene. He played an important part when we regained the Ashes in 1953 and appropriately was batting with Denis Compton when the runs were knocked off in the final Test at The Oval. Hutton also took Edrich to Australia with him in 1954–5, although by this time he was not batting with his old fluency and was certainly not playing as well as in 1950 when he was omitted. However, his technique, his courage, and his experience automatically gained him a place in the Test team.

Bill loved parties and he brought to them the same zest and enthusiasm which epitomized his cricket. He considered that a good one should never end before dawn, and he was always prepared to provide a cabaret act to delay the break-up. His turns were of either the vocal or the conjuring variety. He had acquired his considerable repertoire of songs during long forgotten nights in the Mess and his memory for the lyrics was considerably more impressive than his vocal powers. The Edrich voice was an off-beat, husky whisper which was, however, sufficiently penetrating to reach every corner of the room and from which there was no escape. Two of his most impressive performances were a duet with Len Hutton on the boat out to Australia, when they undertook without a fault, a little tongue-twister on the various accomplishments of Susie and when, at the dinner to celebrate the opening of a new pavilion in Ireland, he substituted four verses of

In Dublin's Fair City for the expected speech and brought the house down. His other favourite party piece involved an egg, a glass of water, a tray, and a broom, which was always far more entertaining when it failed than when it succeeded (except to one distinguished cricket correspondent whose tuxedo never again looked so immaculate).

Bill Edrich, naturally enough, became something of a legend at the Scarborough Festival, which besides producing a great deal of entertaining cricket is, or certainly was, also a non-stop party. Despite the festivities which ran one day into the next, Bill would reel off at least one century per festival with unfailing regularity. The one concession he was prepared to make to the strain of playing nine days cricket with the absolute minimum of sleep was to stand somewhat deeper than usual at slip. On one occasion I suggested to the captain that Bill should come up a few yards to save the single.

It is sometimes forgotten that in his younger days Bill was a more than useful fast bowler, who just before the war was decidedly quick through the air and after the war, when we were admittedly short of pace bowling, sometimes opened the England attack. There was nothing beautiful about his bowling – a short, hurried scurry up to the stumps, followed by a somewhat round arm slinging action (reminiscent of a catapult) with which he propelled the ball with surprising velocity and enormous zeal. His own lack of height, combined with his low action, ensured that he did not achieve a lift that was in any way commensurate with his pace, in fact he tended to skid off the wicket and keep low. He was essentially a shock bowler to be used in short bursts when he was always liable to surprise batsmen with his speed. Injury shortened his career as a fast slinger and he reverted to gentle off-spin. In Minor County Cricket he secured a number of victims in this fashion, but at a higher level his successes were comparatively few. However, just before the Brisbane Test in 1954–5, when it had been decided to enter the match with four 'quick' bowlers – Tyson, Statham, Bedser and myself – I did suggest that we seemed perhaps a shade short of spin and was somewhat surprised to learn that this could be provided by Bill. At that particular time Bill had bowled three overs on the tour which had proved completely unremunerative, except for the fortunate batsman.

Originally a cover point and a very good mover, as one would expect from an ex-professional footballer, Bill gradually developed into an effective and an unspectacular first slip where he held a high percentage of the chances that came his way. He was very agile, but slightly handicapped by the smallness of his hands. His captaincy of Middlesex, and later Norfolk, was similar to his slip fielding, sound rather than showy. He had a wide knowledge of the game and seldom missed a trick. Victory was always his target, but he would fight hard for a draw immediately the odds against victory became too great. As one would expect from a person who enjoyed poker and the races, he was ever willing to take a gamble by an early declaration, or a chase against the clock, if he felt that it was possible to win.

Bill was essentially the type of player to have on the field when there was something at stake. Off the field he was an amusing, indefatigable, sometimes argumentative companion who could be relied upon to liven up most proceedings, a *bon viveur* who would have been in his element in the more riotous days of Hollywood.

5

DENIS COMPTON
The Golden Boy

Of the great English batsmen I have bowled against Denis Compton was the most brilliant and the most unorthodox. When he was set he was not only difficult to dismiss, but his wide and frequently unconventional range of strokes, combined with his ability to improvise, made him difficult to contain. One expects a bad ball to be put away by the class performer, but what any bowler hates is for his good deliveries to be treated in the same fashion. Once, when playing for Middlesex against The Rest at The Oval, Denis, as so often, had advanced down the track to that fine off-spinner, Tom Goddard. He slipped, probably because he had forgotten to re-stud his boots, and fell, yet he not only made contact with the ball but actually hit it to the boundary from his prone position.

Against the faster bowling Compton's initial movement was the same as the majority of the best overseas players, back and across. This was probably due to the fact that he spent his formative years on the hard fast pitches which prevailed at Lord's before the war. Not only were the wickets on the square reliable, but those in the nets there too almost lived up to the ideal of being better than the middle. Once Denis became established however, nets had little appeal for him, except as pre-season looseners, but they played an important part in his early days. Although he is a natural ball player, cricket is not a natural game and like everyone else he had to acquire the fundamentals of batting.

The initial movement back and across, combined with a wonderful eye, quick reactions, a back lift towards third man, and plenty of guts were responsible for his becoming an accomplished hooker and, also meant that he was never unduly worried by great pace. It is interesting that, one of the very few occasions when he was hit by a bouncer – in the 1948 Test at Manchester – was when he was momentarily distracted by the umpire no-balling Ray Lindwall so that his intended hook went off the edge on to his forehead. It was a sickening blow, requiring a number of stitches, and the type of injury to put many players off facing pace bowling for a long time to come. But not Denis. He returned to the battle-field with the score at 119 for 5 and was undefeated with 145 to his credit at the close. At the present time, when there is a shortage of real pace bowling, most batsmen feel undressed unless they are wearing at least one thigh pad; it is a tribute to Denis's outstanding technique that he never bothered with one, even when Lindwall, Miller and Bill Johnston were at their best.

Like all players of genuine class, Denis used his feet well and he was never happier than when going down the pitch to a spinner. In Australia in 1946–7, when many of the English batsmen allowed themselves to be mesmerized by the high-tossed leg-breaks of Colin McCool because they attempted to treat him as a conventional English leg-spinner and play him from the crease, Compton was seldom in trouble.

Some people think of footwork only in terms of going down the wicket, but this is wrong. Correct footwork is one of the founda-tions of batting and is just as essential inside the crease. In this context, when Denis played back he gave himself the maximum amount of time by going right back on to the stumps, so much so that he did on occasions tread on his own wicket.

Perhaps there was a shade too much right hand in Denis's bat-ting, but this did not prevent him driving into the covers with great power, as I found to my cost. This was in my early days with Essex and I allowed myself to be positioned at silly mid-off with Denis batting to the bowling of Peter Smith. I attempted to stop his stroke and the eight stitches I had inserted in the webbing between my two smallest fingers are a permanent reminder of the strength of his off-drive. Even now these fingers open under pres-sure and I have to keep them strapped in the field.

The influence of the right hand was especially noticeable when he used a deadly cover slash to penetrate a packed field. He would not bring his left foot as far across as for the drive, thus giving

The CREAM

himself more room, and he would play the ball, usually on the up, just a shade later.

But the stroke that will always be associated with Denis Compton is the sweep. This can prove dangerous when a fieldsman is stationed between fine and square leg and some thirty yards in from the boundary; indeed in recent years the stroke has been rather over-employed. The South Africans, realizing his fondness for the sweep, planned to trap him this way. Denis overcame the problem because he executed the stroke in a different and more difficult way from most. He played the shot later and made sure of keeping the ball down by hitting it with the bat slanting and not parallel to the ground. In addition he had an almost uncanny ability to place the ball where he desired. At Lord's against Essex I watched him sweep three boundaries off Peter Smith. On the first occasion I was at square leg and the ball went fine. I was moved there and the next took the ball to the exact spot I had vacated. This was the signal for another fieldsman to join me, but it made no difference, as he smote the third to very fine leg.

Denis would have broken even more records during his career, but for the war years and the famous 'knee' which was to restrict his mobility in the later stages. The knee trouble was the result of a football injury received when playing for the Arsenal, with whom he gained a F.A. Cup Medal. He was a very dangerous winger, with a lethal left foot and a born instinct for making and taking goals. Unfairly sometimes he was labelled a lucky footballer, because he had the habit of popping up unexpectedly in just the right spot at just the right moment.

Determination to overcome difficulties has always been one of Denis's outstanding traits and this was never more clearly shown than in the way he refused to allow the 'knee' to end his life as an international cricketer. Despite this considerable handicap which would have caused many to retire, he was still able to make more runs than most completely fit batsmen. He was such a beautiful timer of his strokes and placer of the ball that he could afford to ignore singles and rely mainly on boundaries, but this could make batting with him for the limited performer like myself far more difficult. This was especially noticeable on his last visit to South Africa, when the opposition, knowing his slowness between the wickets, were able to station their fieldsman a shade deeper when he was at the crease.

The golden year for the 'golden boy' was of course 1947, when he scored more runs and more centuries in the season than anyone in the history of the game. At the close of that 'roses, roses all the way' summer I batted with Denis in the Hastings Festival against the South Africans. Thousands turned up in the hope of seeing him complete yet another century and break yet another record. My one fear was that I should run him out – which indeed seemed the only thing that could prevent him achieving this, and was by no means improbable as his calling was unpredictable in the extreme. It has been said that his first call merely meant that he was prepared to open negotiations; while to run out your own brother for nought in his own Benefit match shows little less than genius. Fortunately we managed to avoid calamity on this occasion, largely through some unexpected cooperation from the opposing fieldsmen, but it was a less satisfactory story some years later in a Test Match at Old Trafford. First Denis had me half way down the wicket with his first affirmative, he then halted me there with a frantic 'wait', and finally passed me at full gallop with a confident 'no', with the result that I departed pavilionwards, yet another victim of the Compton three-call trick.

Denis was more than a great batsman; he was essentially an entertainer and one of the biggest of box office draws. The more dour amongst northerners may have regarded with suspicion the almost casual way he tackled the business of amassing runs, but in general he was a source of delight to spectators all over the world; indeed, the feature of his play which I most admired was its gaiety. He not only made batting look easy, he also made it look fun. It contained a mixture of genius, mirth and more than a suggestion of schoolboy impishness, because although he was determined to make runs, he also enjoyed doing it.

Like all natural entertainers he thrived on the large audience and the tense situation. These brought out the best in him, so that he tended to sparkle more brightly in a vital Test at

Melbourne before a capacity crowd than in a comparatively un-important, sparsely attended county match.

Over the years I have been associated in numerous partner-ships with Denis. At international level the first of note occurred in my second Test, against the New Zealanders at Lord's, when we put on 189 for the sixth wicket after the first five had gone for 112. In retrospect, perhaps the most intriguing feature of this stand was that I scored slightly the faster, but that was in the days before I was regarded mainly as a batting limpet.

One of the speediest methods of scoring is for one batsman to cut loose and his colleague to see that he has as much of the strike as possible. Against Pakistan at Nottingham in 1954 I joined Denis when he had already made a century and was in full flow. I de-cided to take a single off the first or second ball whenever I had the strike, and to avoid doing this at the end of an over. The re-sult was that we, or, to be more accurate, Denis, put on 192 in about 100 minutes and the Pakistan attack was sprayed to all parts of the ground with a non-stop assortment of exciting strokes. It was vintage Compton and he went on to his highest score in Test cricket, 278.

One of our most amusing partnerships occurred when I was captaining the M.C.C. against Trinidad. I had opened and de-cided that our best chance of winning was a steady start and then, with plenty of wickets in hand, launch a full scale assault in the final session. Immediately after the tea interval Denis played a maiden and this gave me the opportunity to go up to him and with as serious a face as I could muster, say, 'You stay there, Denis and I'll play the shots'. I hurriedly retreated to the other end be-fore the full significance of my remark registered, slogged twenty or so while he was recovering and then departed to the pavilion happy that, with Denis in control, we would beat Trinidad for the first time for a long while.

However, although Denis has a sunny disposition I have on some occasions made him angry. Once when he was well set for Middlesex, I decided that I would contain him by some defensive leg theory. As I was only employing this against him and not the lesser players he became even more incensed. Another time, at

Colchester, he was within reach of a superb hundred before lunch, when he allowed himself to be bowled round his legs by my round-arm slinger, a fate worse than death for any batsman, let alone for a master in complete control!

In 1950 Denis went to Australia as vice-captain of the M.C.C. He had led the Players well and many felt that he might well make an ideal leader in the future, but it did not work out that way. Although he was generally regarded with great affection, he did not make a good captain, because in times of stress he was apt to become either slightly petulant or would temporarily lose interest. When he was captaining Middlesex I remember him telling that accurate left-hander, Jack Young, to toss the ball up. Each time he did so the batsmen, who were on the attack, promptly smote it to the boundary and the sufferer was not surprisingly incensed. Years later I went with the International Cavaliers to Jamaica under Denis after he had retired and then he did a splendid job in every sense and even scored a century with an innings which contained much of the old Compton magic.

Denis was also, of course, a useful left arm 'chinaman' and googly bowler. He spun the ball considerably, but he lacked discipline and singleness of purpose. Although he was capable of producing the unplayable delivery his length and direction tended to be wayward so that he was apt to prove expensive.

Until increasing age and the handicap of the knee reduced his mobility, Denis was a brilliant and decidedly unpredictable fieldsman. Whenever the game became dull and he was out in the country, he had a tendency to wander both physically and mentally. This trait certainly increased the problems of the captain who, unless he was constantly on the alert, was liable to find that Denis had moved far from his original station. In these circumstances there was much to be said for having him near the bat where he held some magnificent catches. He liked to stand closer to the wicket than most, because he believed it was better to risk the chance of putting down a catch through being too near than being too deep and the chance failing to carry. His reactions were, of course, very quick and enabled him to bring off some remarkable catches, especially with his left hand, which he made appear simple.

Quite apart from his ability, Denis would always be one of my first choices for any overseas tour, because so much of the fun of his batting was reflected in a naturally happy and uncomplex character. He is an easy, pleasant companion who enjoys life and is generous in deed and outlook. One may disagree with some of his views which are normally very uncomplicated but it is difficult to believe that anyone who knows him well could dislike him as an individual. He is extremely good looking, and few people I have encountered have possessed so much natural charm, a charm which appealed to young and old, male and female, and friend and foe. He was always remarkably modest and a splendid mixer in any company.

It is comparatively easy to be a first class tourist when one is enjoying a successful trip, but I was with Denis in Australia in 1950–1 during one of his rare periods of failure. It is still difficult to believe that he had a Test batting average of only seven, yet despite the disappointments on the field and some domestic problems, he still retained both his perspective and his sense of fun, a man who was always able to share a joke with anyone and could laugh at himself.

Of course Denis has never been famed for his punctuality, reliability and sense of responsibility. Who but Denis would have to be told by a policeman on point duty that the Test Match was due to start half an hour earlier and that he was already late? Or before the start of an international at Hampden Park when all the other players were changed and ready to go out on to the field, realize that he needed some studs in his boots? Inevitably these frailties led to some minor disagreements with the authorities but, as an official once remarked, 'You cannot possibly be cross with Denis for long'.

My own affection for Denis was increased by the fact that we were kindred spirits in being untidy. Nobody is ever keen to change next to me in the dressing room, because I tend to spread and at the end of the match my bag is liable to contain a miscellaneous collection of odd socks, gloves and shirts that have somehow found their way there. Our colleagues always believed that Denis and I should be near. This was to cost me dear in the West Indies as he once took out my bat by mistake and proceeded to make a hundred with it, so that I lost it for good! Even now I occasionally find myself putting on a pair of socks with the name Compton on them and it was not very long ago that I saw him sporting a tie which looked decidedly familiar.

While we were touring the Caribbean we used to share the same room and I learned the full extent of his aptitude for disorganization. By the time we had both unpacked it resembled one of those film sets after the crook has made an intensive search for the missing treasure without putting anything back.

At one time the disorganized chaos which surrounded Compton extended to his business life. He has always wanted to help people and this became a distinct problem, as he was reluctant to turn down the numerous invitations which kept arriving. The outcome was that he would suddenly discover that he had agreed to attend three functions which were all taking place on the same date, at the same time and at different places. To increase the problem Denis received an enormous amount of fan mail which would have taxed the ingenuity of a first class secretary, while he could by no stretch of the imagination be termed an inveterate letter writer. Inevitably business correspondence, private correspondence and fan mail became inextricably jumbled in the dressing rooms of the world. Lord's was littered with Compton letters, until Bagenal Harvey, who was later to exert so much influence in various sporting fields, took charge of his affairs. At the time Bagenal was with a book publishing firm and by chance Denis gave him a lift in his car from a cricket match. The methodical Bagenal was horrified by the conglomeration of paper that filled the Compton car, and casually remarked that his business manager must have a great deal of work to do. The amount Bagenal did not fully appreciate until he found himself pressed into service and the following week Denis arrived with two cabin trunks filled with a miscellaneous collection of letters, bills, invitations and uncashed cheques. This was to be the start of a long friendship and a working relationship which proved a happy arrangement in all

50

respects. Bagenal systematically removed the chaos, straightened out the many difficulties, and in addition made his new client a considerable amount of money by sensibly exploiting his worth commercially, so that today Denis Compton Ltd is a financially sound, prosperous business concern with many interests.

Not only did Denis possess the golden touch on the cricket and football fields, but it was with him on most other occasions. One hesitates to play cards with him, not because of any outstanding skill in this direction, simply because he nearly always manages to pick up a strong hand. He is one of those people who receive tips that really come home and whose putts will tremble on the brink before dropping in. One day I went racing with him at Sydney which was to provide a classic example of this lucky streak of his. For once the magic was failing to work and in an effort to recoup his losses Denis decided to have a tenner on the final race. The friendly bookmaker advised him against his selection, suggested horse number seven, and proceeded to scrawl out a quite indecipherable ticket which he handed to Denis. A few pre-race enquiries elicited the information that the mysterious number seven was merely a country hack without a chance. However, this did not stop it romping home by some sixth lengths at ten to one.

After the race, Denis approached the bookie somewhat circumspectly as he was by no means certain whether he was in fact on the winner. He need not have worried. He was paid out £100 with a friendly smile and 'didn't I tell you so?' We were on our way back to the car with the happy prospect of a dinner on Compton, when suddenly there was a shout of 'Denis'. Sprinting towards us was a short, stout man, sweating abundantly from the unusual exercise. On reaching us he apologized profusely for having omitted to pay back the stake money and handed over another tenner.

When a professional bookmaker does not take your money for your original choice, tips you the winner, accepts the bet, pays out contentedly, and then chases you half a mile to give you a further £10, you must possess exceptional charm and rightly deserve the tag of 'golden', twenty-four carat!

6

WEEKES, WORRELL AND WALCOTT
The 'W' Formation

For more than a decade West Indian batting strength revolved round the W formation. Seldom, if ever, has one country – let alone one small semi-tropical island, Barbados – possessed three middle order batsmen of the calibre of Weekes, Worrell and Walcott. But apart from their hunger for runs and the same place of origin the three Ws had little else in common. They were not built alike, they did not look alike and their cricketing methods were dissimilar.

Everton Weekes was a small, neat, compact back-foot player, who possessed such a wonderful range of attacking strokes that bowling to him on a hard, fast, true wicket could become something of a nightmare. In addition he possessed a superb defence and he was probably the most complete batsman of the three Ws. He spent a number of summers in the Lancashire League where he was an enormous success as player, coach and as a person. One result was that he became a better technician on a bad wicket than any other West Indian, with the possible exception of George Headley. There were, in fact, certain similarities between George and Everton – both were short and favoured the back foot, although George was rather more open in his stance, but George never had the same amount of support from his colleagues. In his prime, to all intents and purposes he *was* the West Indian batting.

In 1967 I played with Everton Weekes in a Sunday Cavaliers match. It so happened that some of the best young prospects in England were taking part in the game, and although he had retired, was over here on holiday and out of practice and in borrowed gear, he clearly dwarfed all the other batsmen in ability, if not in size, as he produced a series of masterly strokes; these included a hook which sent the ball scudding along the ground

52

to the mid-wicket boundary and a straight six, struck effortlessly over the sight screen off the back foot. However, nothing impressed the young English players more than the certainty with which he pulverized the bad ball.

As one would expect from his build, Everton was very nimble on his feet. This enabled him to be in a position to hook the pace men early, while often he refused to allow the slow bowlers to bounce. His cross-bat strokes were particularly crisp and devastating, although the hook led to his downfall on occasions, particularly when he was touring Australia. The Australian captain noted his partiality for this stroke and had Lindwall and Miller unleash a number of bouncers at him. Everton predictably accepted the challenge with the result that he holed out on several occasions to Neil Harvey, a superlative out-field who had been especially stationed on the deep fine leg boundary.

One of the most spectacular and technically brilliant knocks which Everton produced against England occurred at Lord's on his second tour in 1957. The pitch was untrustworthy, lively with an uneven bounce and ideal for seamers who could also obtain considerable lateral deviation. Although handicapped by injury he played an innings which would have been noteworthy for its tempo and its strokes on the most perfect wicket in Barbados.

A large score by Everton which I did not enjoy was in the fourth Test at Trinidad on the mat. He was in his thirties and looking ominously sound when he made one of his very rare mistakes. I was bowling off a short run, with the keeper Dick Spooner, in place of the injured Godfrey Evans, standing up to the stumps and my fieldsmen thinking more in terms of preventing runs than holding catches. I bowled a ball just short of a length a fraction wide of the off stump and managed to achieve a shade more bounce than Everton expected. He unleashed his lethal square cut but managed a top edge which was very well taken by Dick. We naturally appealed exultantly and then to my dismay and indignation it was turned down by the umpire. To make matters worse the white coated official made the mistake of trying to explain his decision. He said that he had heard of it, but had failed to see the deviation off the bat. As Spooner was standing up to the

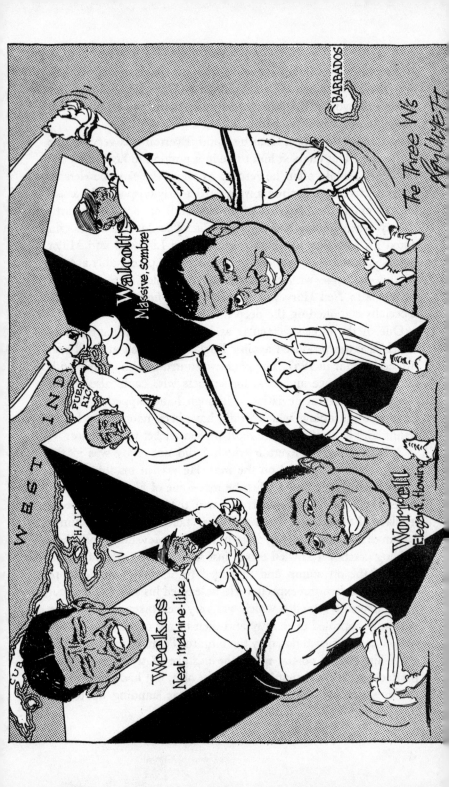

stumps and the ball travelled at the most twelve inches after hitting the bat, this was hardly surprising. When, much, much later, I caught Everton off Tony Lock he had taken his score to 206. Throughout that innings my mind kept flashing back to the flash and edge when he was in his thirties. Obviously one has to accept these quirks of fate, but it is not easy for a bowler on a pitch like that after he has taken nought for over a hundred. However, Everton's innings in the following Test was much more satisfactory. He played back to a delivery from me which nipped back off the seam far more than either of us expected and his off stump went somersaulting back to the keeper before he had opened his account.

Everton's square cut had an authoritarian ring and he loved to 'hit de ball on de rise'. Like all the great players he had the ability to take boundaries with a straight bat off both the front and the back foot, although he preferred to be on the latter. On one occasion in the West Indies Brian Statham produced one of his very few over-pitched deliveries. Len Hutton, for example, would have hit it through the covers off the front foot, but Everton preferred to play the shot a shade later off his back foot. The ball reached the boundary without a fieldsman having the opportunity to move because the timing was so sweet.

The quick reactions which were so valuable to Everton as a batsman were an equal asset in the field. He was an outstanding slip who had the ability to make the most difficult catches appear simple. I once snicked a ball low and fast with the wicket-keeper standing up and obscuring Everton who was at first slip, I was just about to congratulate myself on a lucky four when to my dismay Everton merely stooped and plucked the ball up only inches from the ground. Without flurry or flamboyance he had brought off one of the most difficult types of catch there is in the game. In the League it was necessary for him to turn his arm over as well as providing a high proportion of his side's total. In this class of cricket he was quite a useful performer with the ball, but at high levels he was only regarded as a friendly, merely occasional bowler.

The average West Indian by nature and environment is a

happy, easy-going individual. Everton enjoys his life, and one always feels better for having been in his company. His outlook has remained fundamentally unsophisticated, uncomplicated and untroubled by inhibitions. His experiences in all parts of the world have matured him, given him additional self-confidence, and removed much of his original shyness, but they have not altered his inborn modesty or his honesty.

Great players frequently make indifferent coaches, for genius is largely a matter of inspiration which cannot be transmitted, while frequently they are too impatient or self-centred. However, Everton is an exception, and Barbados cricket owes much to him. In addition to his extensive knowledge and love of the game, the secret of his success with the young cricketers lies in his genuine interest in them, combined with an inborn kindness and sympathy. As a result Everton has become almost father figure to numerous Barbadians, many of whom are now established internationals. They instinctively go to him for advice, not only on the game itself, but on everything.

There was sometimes a machine-like quality about Everton Weekes' batting which reminded me of Sir Donald Bradman – a superlative run-getter, effective rather than beautiful. The late Sir Frank Worrell, on the other hand, was the most artistic and stylish member of this triumvirate. Tall and loosely built, he possessed a smoothness of movement and a feline grace which made him fascinating to watch whether batting, bowling or fielding. He made everything appear effortless and natural. His backlift was high and preceded a fully flowing follow through. Although he hit the ball very hard he gave the impression of almost caressing it. His strokes had a wristy flavour and a delicacy of touch which charmed all those who saw him in action. There was poetry in his batting.

I especially remember one stroke he played against Alec Bedser in the second Test match at Lord's in 1950. For once the 'big fella' bowled a full half-volley outside the off stump. Many players would have scored four off that particular delivery, but very few would have had the ability, or the instinct to reach the boundary via an exquisite late cut. This was genuine West Indian magic and vintage Worrell.

Frankie was apt to be slightly vulnerable against real pace at the commencement of an innings, and in general he played the slower better than the faster bowlers. For one thing they gave him more chance to demonstrate his driving. When he was in the mood it was unprofitable, if not impossible, for a spinner to operate against him. What does a bowler do against a batsman who goes down the pitch and drives good length deliveries through the covers to the boundary and then goes on to his back foot and hits the slightly shorter ball, with no apparent effort, for six over the sight screen?

Like so many West Indian cricketers Frank Worrell spent a considerable time in the Lancashire League and while there he also took a degree at Manchester University. He soon fathomed the intricacies of the English wicket and learned to adapt his play accordingly with the result that he tightened up his defence which was always basically sound because of the essential correctness of his technique. This was to prove especially valuable on his last (1963) tour to England as captain of the West Indies when a knee injury had curtailed some of his freedom of movement. It meant that when a difficult situation arose he was just the right person to effect a recovery. However, he always remained at his best on the hard, fast wickets of the Caribbean where he could afford to drive along the carpet on the up without fear of the ball deviating off the track, or keeping low.

In his early days he was avaricious for runs, amassed some enormous scores and took part in several record-breaking partnerships, but as time went by he became more willing to settle for a century. I shall always remember with mixed feelings his prolonged stand with Everton Weekes on the mat at Trinidad, probably the truest and most perfect pitch on which I ever bowled. Strangely enough, Weekes and Worrell, like Sobers and Kanhai, were not associated in as many long partnerships as might have been expected, though in the long run this may have been to the advantage of the West Indies for whenever one failed the other had a habit of succeeding. This occasion was to prove an exception. They came together with the scoreboard showing 92 for 2 and when the next wicket fell the total had reached 430. Throughout this massive stand Frankie never gave the slightest chance or ever looked as if he might make a mistake. Runs literally flowed from the bats of these two superb artists, and all the bowlers by the end had been reduced to mere hacks, and to thinking that a maiden was something of a triumph!

Worrell was an able left-arm bowler, who could operate as an orthodox slow left-armer or at medium fast. In normal circumstances he was a better performer in the latter role. Because of a shortage of West Indian pace bowlers in his early days Frankie was frequently called upon to open their attack when strictly speaking his best role was as third seamer. He had an easy, almost languid approach to the wicket and a fluent action. His pace was never above a fast medium but he could, when riled, and this was a rare event, produce a respectable if hardly a devastating bouncer. He was at his best with the new ball which he could move, mainly into the batsman, late and effectively. At international level he was a useful rather than a great bowler who had the advantage of being a little quicker and more dangerous than he appeared on the surface. As a fieldsman, until his knee injury, he was invaluable because he was a fine performer in any position.

Although Frankie was such a fine all round cricketer the most important contribution that he made to West Indian, and indeed, world cricket was not as a performer, but rather as a captain. To appreciate the full significance of what he achieved it is necessary to understand something about the islands themselves and how the game is controlled in the Caribbean. To begin, the four main centres – Barbados, Jamaica, Trinidad and Guyana – all have very different histories so that it follows that the outlook, tradition, and background varies considerably. Nor are they close-knit. Jamaica is some 1,500 miles from Barbados, and even their cricket seasons are not identical. As a result considerable rivalry and sometimes even active dislike exists. In the past players were often chosen for international matches in the West Indies not on ability alone, but because they happened to belong to the centre which was staging the Test. This did not make life easy for the captain who, in addition to not necessarily having the best possible side at his disposal, also had to overcome the prejudice of being white while the majority of his players were coloured. In consequence the players tended to look upon themselves first as Jamaicans, or Trinidadians, and secondly as West Indians.

Frankie changed all that when he was given the captaincy of the West Indian side that toured Australia in 1960–1. Although he lost the series, never has Australia been more enthusiastic about a team, and never has a captain been so universally acclaimed. When they arrived they were unsung and underrated. Nobody gave them any chance and nobody was especially interested, but Frankie and his side caught the imagination, played some truly magnificent cricket, and rekindled a love for the game which had begun to fade. When they departed their send-off was magnificent, moving and completely deserved.

In 1963 Worrell led the West Indies to England for another highly popular tour, only this time he had the additional satisfaction of returning with the rubber even if his personal contribution as a player was less.

What made Frankie such a great captain? First and foremost he really understood the intricacies of the West Indian situation and the volatile nature of the players under his command. He knew the many jealousies that existed between the islands and realized the importance of his party becoming a complete unit. So often in the past West Indian sides had merely been a collection of talented individuals, sub-divided into small cliques. Because of their ability they had been impressive when things were running smoothly, but had often proved vulnerable under stress. Under Frankie they became a real team and eventually the finest side in the world.

Secondly, Frankie was coloured which automatically gave him the whole-hearted support of the majority of West Indians and the press. It also brought him much closer to his own players. He was one of them. They could use him as a model and attempt to emulate him in a way which was never possible with a white captain.

Thirdly, Frankie was a very astute technician. He was only too happy to give the impression (and he understood the value of a good image) that all West Indian cricketers were gay, exciting and colourful, but he never allowed this to interfere with his main concern, winning matches. He appreciated the necessity of a 'sheet anchor' and used Conrad Hunte very effectively in this vital role. He knew when it paid to set a tight field and was not prepared to attack when this was the wrong course or the odds were not favourable. After all cricket is essentially a game of ebb and flow. The most exciting moments are the outcome of the situation, and may well have nothing to do with run rates.

Fourthly, he was fortunate in having a very fine group of players whom, because of his experience and ability, he was able to help in a practical way. In the Lord's Test in 1963 Basil Butcher started to become over-excited as he neared his hundred. From the other end Frankie was able to calm him down.

Finally, he possessed the ideal personality for the job. His charm was enormous, made all the more effective because it was genuine and effortless. I remember Ray Smith coming back to Essex after a Commonwealth tour to India and almost his first remark to me was on how much Worrell had contributed to the enjoyment of everybody in the party. He certainly understood his West Indians, their needs, their strengths and their weaknesses. He inspired their confidence. They respected him as a cricketer, admired him as a captain and loved him as a man. This devotion I can fully understand, because I had the opportunity of getting to know both Frankie and his side rather better than most. I had, of course, played against him regularly in Test cricket, but it was not until much later that we became friends. During the winter following Frank Worrell's triumphant tour of England I went to Jamaica with the International Cavaliers. Frankie was then living in Jamaica and captained the island against us in a highly entertaining series of matches. He was a magnificent, delightfully casual host, who was aided by an exceptionally charming wife. One evening we were quietly sipping rum – why does rum always taste so much better in the West Indies than it does at home? – when he casually remarked how he wanted to make one more short trip to England with his boys. From this remark was born a trip the following summer which later was to develop into the annual Rothman's 'World Series'. I was invited to look after the West Indies – seldom have I had such an easy and pleasant job, which gave me a unique opportunity to understand and appreciate the spell which Frankie had cast over his players.

In the entire history of the game there can have been very few better captains, and certainly there has never been a more popular one. Very seldom have I encountered anyone with such a delightful personality and such a sunny disposition – which makes his sudden and early death an even bigger loss. When I went to Westminster Abbey to pay my last respects, I could not help thinking of the waste. What a wonderful ambassador he would have made in England or Australia. He was a natural. Cricket had lost one of her finest players and I had lost a friend. He has, however, left me a host of treasured memories, a cover drive in which technical perfection was surpassed by beauty and power; catching him in the slips, playing head tennis in the sea, drinking rum and coconut water; his sense of fun and that infectious sparkling laugh. My epitaph would be that he helped to make the world a sunnier place.

Clyde Walcott's batting was in keeping with his build – massive and powerful. He was not as complete as Everton Weekes nor as graceful as Frank Worrell, but of all three Ws I found bowling to Clyde on a good wicket the most difficult and unremunerative. He had the ability to hit good length deliveries with astonishing ferocity using a straight bat off both front and back foot. Drop the ball just a fraction short and back it would come so hard that, unless the bowler, or fieldsman, were unlucky enough to be in the way, it was inevitably a boundary. Exactly the same thing happened if the ball was slightly over-pitched, except that then Clyde would belt it off his front foot.

The most remarkable maiden over I ever bowled was against Clyde Walcott. This occurred during his superb innings of 220 against England at Barbados. My first delivery was straight, of a full length, and would have hit the middle stump, if Clyde had not driven it like a bullet off his front foot. Only a superb piece of fielding prevented the deserved four. My second delivery was identical in every way except that it was just a fraction shorter. Clyde's reply was identical except that he smote this one off his back foot and short extra, with remarkable agility, stopped the four. The process was repeated each ball throughout that memorable over. What it amounted to was that I bowled six balls as well as I was able with every delivery hitting the middle, or the middle and off stumps before the intervention of Clyde's bat, but only six superb pieces of fielding prevented him scoring 24 runs. He thumped the very best I could offer alternately off his back and front foot and, although each delivery was hit on the rise they all travelled along the floor.

Clyde possessed a remarkably high and looping backlift which certainly would not have appealed to a purist. It was so high and looped that one always felt that he ought to be a candidate for a fast yorker, especially at the commencement of an innings, but strangely he never appeared to have difficulty in stopping one, even when delivered by Brian Statham. He illustrated very clearly that it does not matter how the bat is picked up, providing it is brought down fast and straight, while the higher the backlift, the harder the ball can be struck.

For such a big, heavy man, Clyde was surprisingly light and agile on his feet, and he was never worried by slow bowlers with a teasing flight. Like most Barbadians reared on fast, true pitches, he liked to attack and, though impetuosity sometimes led to his downfall, it usually paid off in terms of entertainment and runs. However, this did not mean that Clyde had an indifferent defensive technique – indeed it is impossible to become a great, or even a good, batsman without one. Over the years I bowled against Clyde on a number of helpful wickets, when the ball moved around the air and off the seam, and the way he carefully watched every delivery, but was still prepared to despatch the bad one to the boundary was an object lesson to any young cricketer. In particular, I remember him scoring 50 for the West Indies out of a total of only 115 against Essex on a seam bowling paradise at Valentine's Park. This was a masterly innings which saved his side from rout and almost certain defeat. What was especially impressive was the way he middled the ball which had deviated sharply. Like Weekes and Worrell, he undoubtedly learned how to play under these conditions during his stay in the Lancashire League.

The best hookers of really fast bowling are normally small, neat, compact men, like Sir Donald Bradman, Everton Weekes, or Lindsay Hassett, simply because they are in position that fraction earlier; but Clyde played the hook superbly and with tremendous power. In 1951-2 he had an unhappy tour of Australia, when the pace of the Australians clearly undermined his confidence as it did that of most of the West Indian batsmen, but he was to extract an ample revenge four years later in the West Indies when, despite being on the losing side, he scored 827 runs, and was the outstanding and most effective of the three Ws.

When the West Indies arrived in England in 1950 under John Goddard, Weekes and Worrell were already household names, but Walcott was comparatively unknown. He was selected for the tour as a wicket-keeper-batsman, and it was not until the second Test match at Lord's that it was appreciated that the W twins had developed into triplets. I was injured and unable to take part but watched the match from the pavilion. At one time in their second innings, the West Indians were in danger of collapsing but Walcott soon transformed the situation with an innings of power and authority. He made 168 not out and collared our attack in a way which made me thankful I was not performing.

Perhaps because the ball does not beat the bat nearly as often as in this country, West Indian wicket-keepers are often adequate rather than exceptional. Even so, and despite his bulk, Walcott was remarkably nimble, and, considering his lack of experience, took the two spinners, Ramadhin and Valentine, well; however, he was never more than of reasonable standard and not surprisingly he decided after this tour to concentrate on his batting. His decision was more than justified by the marked increase in his batting powers.

However his spell behind the stumps had helped him in 'picking' slow bowlers and he could not understand why English batsmen had so much difficulty in deciphering which was Ramadhin's leg-break. I was sitting in the pavilion with Clyde at Southend one time while Ramadhin was bowling, and he nominated each delivery with complete certainty. As time went on it became easier to 'pick' Ramadhin but on that first trip I had to rely on an instinct which was not always right!

Few batsmen have been able to match Clyde Walcott's power and majesty. To drive the ball clean out of the ground is a comparatively rare feat, yet Clyde could do this off his back foot. What was even more surprising was the effectiveness of his sweeping. Give him a ball just outside the leg stump, and in a moment he would be down on one knee sweeping viciously. Such was the energy he put into the stroke that in the rare event of his getting a top edge it was still likely to carry for six.

In company with all the West Indians I have played cricket against, Clyde had a marked sense of humour although this simmered rather than perpetually bubbled. In temperament he was more reserved, quieter and less effervescent than the other two Ws. At times he seemed somewhat suspicious. The years have mellowed him and he has done a fine job as coach in Guyana despite many difficulties that exist because of the feeling that prevails between those of Indian and of African extraction. He must take much of the credit for the marked improvement in cricket in Guyana since he took up residence there.

One final memory of Clyde Walcott, which illustrates the majesty of his batting. The bowler sent down a medium paced delivery just short of a length. Clyde went back, there was the full swing of the bat with that extra waggle at the end and the ball was sent soaring high over mid off into the very back of that stand which overlooks the delightful ground in Barbados. I doubt if any other player could have played that particular stroke, and certainly nobody with such ease.

The W formation represented all the very best features of West Indian batting, the compact efficiency of Weekes, the effortless grace of Worrell and the majesty and power of Walcott. All three were great players in their own right, and all three could have commanded a place in a World XI, but as a unit they were unique. Different though they were in technique, temperament and style, they were as one in the fundamentals. First, they all possessed the ability to despatch the good ball to the boundary and were therefore difficult to contain even when the bowling was accurate. Secondly, they were all able to strike the ball on the rise but still keep it on the ground. This is a skill which is all too rare in English first class cricket today. Perhaps we have too much coaching in how to hit the bad ball and stop the good. This is fine in the early stages, always assuming the pupil is not discouraged from also hitting the good if he possesses the ability. Later it might well pay to have him scoring off length bowling as otherwise he is liable to find himself tied down when he has to face a class bowler. Thirdly, the Ws were able, when in the mood, to indulge in a run riot against even a powerful international attack. Fourthly, they were all run hungry and were only too delighted to carry on amassing runs after they had completed their first hundred. Fifthly, their batting contained the fun and fire which is the hallmark of Barbadian cricket. It was full of charm and may have appeared carefree to the spectator, but it was never careless because all three were professionals. The fact that they were West Indians made them enjoy their work so much more than many English players seem to do and this consequently increased the pleasure of the spectators. It was both an experience and a privilege to bowl against them all when they were in their prime.

c

7

TOM GRAVENEY

Mr Elegance

The recall of Tom Graveney to the England team against the West Indies in 1966, after years in the wilderness when he was written off as not up to the required standard and indeed over the hill, proved to be an unqualified success. It was not only a romantic move, but a logical one, because nearly everyone in the game, other than the selectors apparently, knew Tom to be the most dependable batsman in the country, and that he ought to have been picked several seasons earlier. What our selectors had failed to appreciate, until it was almost too late, was that, once Graveney had settled down at Worcester, he became a far more consistent player than he had ever been in the past. He has always been a very fine batsman, but with maturity he became a great one.

Tom reached his peak in 1964, when Worcester won the title for the first time. Although Middlesex in 1947 were an exception, the Championship is decided mainly by bowlers; however, it is doubtful whether one single batsman has ever exerted as much influence on the Championship as did Graveney for Worcester that year; he elegantly bestrode the scene that summer and without him his county could never have triumphed. He carried Worcester's batting, scoring well over 2,000 runs, hitting numerous centuries, and making fourteen other scores of over 50. However, it was not only the runs he scored, but the number of occasions he steered his side to a reasonable total when the pressure was on and the pitch was poor. Against Essex on a lively wicket Tom made 106 out of 229, and because of that fine innings, which was beyond the capabilities of practically any other English player, Worcester won the match.

This was a typical example of the mastery he exerted, but our selectors omitted him while we lost the Ashes to one of the poorest Australian teams to visit this country. It did not make sense at the time, and in retrospect appears even more nonsensical. The final irony of Tom's belated recall to international cricket was that, afterwards, he was chosen on merit to play for the World XI in Barbados. Yet he had not been considered good enough to be even a member of three M.C.C. parties who toured Australia and South Africa, when he was in fact batting better than he had ever done!

I first met Tom Graveney when Essex went to play on the lovely school ground at Cheltenham which has a beautiful batting wicket. This match became stamped in my memory because the luncheon interval was lengthened and enlivened by a remarkable speech. The orator, a local dignitary, commenced by telling everyone, and apologizing for the fact, that mediocrity was the outstanding feature of both teams. He went on to say that Gloucester had done nothing of note since the prewar days of Walter Hammond. The Gloucester skipper, Basil Allen, was, not surprisingly, very, very incensed, as only two years previously his team had failed to carry off the Championship by the narrowest of margins. The speaker continued by welcoming us, 'the men from Exeter', and then was generous enough to suggest that there was an element of hope for both the sides. Gloucester, for example, possessed two promising young cricketers, 'The Brothers Gravity'. From that day I always thought of Tom as 'Gravity'.

On the field I was immediately impressed by Tom's style and also noticed that high flowing backlift which suggested that he might be susceptible to the bouncer. In those days he was comparatively naïve, accepted my challenge, and swished at a head-high delivery which later he would have contemptuously ignored. The result was a catch at the wicket. I need hardly add that Tom was to take his revenge on numerous occasions in the years ahead; I have lost count of the number of centuries he has made against Essex for both Gloucester and Worcester, not to mention the fifties.

My first of many tours with Tom Graveney was to the West Indies in 1953–4, and it was then that I really began to know

His Elegance
Tom Graveney C.B.E.

him as a person and not merely as a talented batsman from another county. We both liked hot weather and beautiful beaches, rum and Coke and impromptu parties. We were both fascinated by the calypsos, though Tom sang them rather better. We both were keen, though far from expert bridge players and on the way back from the Caribbean once played from 9 am until 2 am with breaks only for refreshments. We were both prepared to go on to the golf course, but here the similarity ended because Tom is an exceptionally fine golfer with an exquisite swing who would have done really well if he had decided to concentrate on that sport instead of cricket.

Subsequent tours, both official and unofficial, increased my regard for him both as a player and as an individual. We have shared moments of triumph, such as when we retained the Ashes at Adelaide in 1954–5, and we have also shared moments of disappointment, like in 1958, though the main reason for our failure then was not the bent-arm controversy but the fact that we failed to play to our potential or as a team. However, above all else both of us have extracted enormous pleasure from touring and playing cricket.

Every time I see Tom at the crease one adjective immediately comes to mind: elegant. There have been few, if any, English players more attractive to watch over the past decade. Everything about his batting is graceful. It starts with his stance which is easy, upright and unmistakable. He has a top-of-the-handle grip, his backlift is high, his timing delicate, and he follows through with a flourish. This high backlift did on occasions prove his undoing against fast bowling in the early stages of his career in Test cricket, but it is also one of the main reasons why he possesses so much appeal for the spectator. A drive by a person with a short backlift may be as effective as one by Tom, but it never can be as exciting to watch. A cover drive by him, with full, graceful arc, represents considerably more than four runs; it is a thing of beauty, to be remembered and treasured.

But the most handsome batsmen do not always make the most runs. In county cricket Tom Graveney has always been a prolific scorer, but in Test cricket, when the going was hard, he was not

always as successful as his ability warranted. When we toured
Australia under Sir Leonard Hutton, Tom did not really come
into his own until the end of the tour. In the final Test, with the
series already decided, he scored a wonderful 100, while in the
New Zealand Tests he overshadowed everyone with a series of
innings of exceptional merit and brilliance. Technically, apart
from a tendency to hit across the line when scoring on the leg
side, Tom has always been a very correct player. What then, was
the reason for his comparative failure at international level, until
his triumphant reappearance on the international scene against
the West Indies?

I have an idea that in his early days his temperament unconsciously resented the restrictions which have inevitably become
part of so many Test battles whenever the opposition possesses a
top-class attack. The knowledge that he could not afford to make
a mistake affected his reactions so that he was unable to play his
normal game. In the second Test of 1954 at Barbados he was at
the crease for a very long time with little effect, and his tempo
made even myself appear to be a fast scorer. On a beautiful track
he forgot all his shots and allowed himself to be contained by two
accurate spinners, Ramadhin and Valentine, who were not
achieving much turn. It was a classic example of a player allowing
a situation (we were facing a huge total) to blind his better judgement. In county and festival matches he has always looked truly
Olympian so that it was difficult to understand why in a number
of internationals he has appeared human and vulnerable.

Tom improved as a batsman after he left his native Gloucester.
He had been appointed their captain and proved to be an adequate rather than an outstanding leader, perhaps because he
tried to please everyone which is nearly always a fatal policy. At
the time he was – other than as a maker of runs – comparatively
inexperienced and in some respects rather naïve, while the idea
of a professional skipper was only reluctantly being accepted by
the county's hierarchy. In 1960 Tom led Gloucester, who had an
undistinguished summer, although despite an injury, he comfortably headed their batting averages. At the end of the season the
Gloucester committee decided to replace him by an amateur,

C. T. M. Pugh, who possessed a strictly limited knowledge of the first class game. Understandably this was a bitter personal blow to his pride and, predictably, he resigned and decided to go elsewhere. I ran into him London at this time and did my best to try to persuade him to settle his differences with his county, but to no avail. I gained the impression that the whole unfortunate business might have been avoided if only a little more tact and foresight had been employed, but this has seldom been an outstanding characteristic of county committees. Gloucester were naturally reluctant to release their most talented cricketer and this meant that he was forced to waste an entire season before he became eligible to play for Worcester. The undercurrents and the inevitable wrangling, publicity, accusation and counter-accusation left their mark on a basically uncomplicated, easy-going individual so that when Tom reappeared on the first-class scene it seemed that some of the fun in his batting had been replaced by an increased determination to score runs. He quickly settled down to become the most consistent player in the country. Thus a new, harder, more ruthless Graveney was born, but because of his style he remained a delight to spectators everywhere.

Of all the outstanding batsmen I have bowled against none has been as predominantly front-foot as Tom. This characteristic was encouraged by two factors. First, many of the Gloucester pitches on which he was trained were inclined to be slow and to take spin. In these conditions there is much to be said in favour of being on the front foot. Secondly, Tom is tall and his height enabled him to ride a delivery which rose sharply even when on the front foot. Against fast bowling Tom largely employs a half-cock shot with the weight on his leading leg. To overcome the problem of scoring against a pace bowler who keeps the ball just short of the length he has, in addition to nudging and running the ball, developed a semi-push, semi-drive on the up, played late with the weight on his front foot; it is a most effective, highly individual and rewarding stroke.

What one first notices when bowling to Tom is his left leg thrusting firmly forward. It used to irritate me that if I managed to make a ball come back sufficiently to beat his very broad bat, it did not hit the wicket because the pad was in the way and my frantic appeal for lbw was seldom of any avail. It is interesting to note that he is so expert on the front foot that he is even able to hook quick bowling from there. The one discernible weakness in his method is that it makes him slightly vulnerable to a top-class off-spinner, at least at the start of an innings. I always feel that there is a chance of having him caught out in the forward leg position, particularly if the ball should stop a little because this may well increase the influence of his right hand and because he tends to follow through even when playing defensively.

Like all great batsmen he has a wide variety of strokes, but relies largely on scoring his runs with straight bat shots in an arc between extra cover and forward short leg. This is the safest and surest method as one is employing the full face of the bat and is less likely to edge the ball.

In his younger days Tom was an extremely fine all-round fieldsman, better than average in most positions and possessing a very good pair of hands. As a slip, in his prime I would rate him as outstanding without ever quite attaining true greatness. In the deep he has always been reliable and takes the high catch baseball fashion with the hands reversed and the knowledge that if he fails to close them in time he will be hit on the forehead. He is an occasional bowler, whose most dangerous ball is the leg-break which does not turn.

One performance of Tom Graveney's against Essex at Romford many years ago gives a good indication of his batting mastery. On that occasion the wicket was so green that it would have served as a natural advertisement for an artificial fertilizer and the ball moved about in a most bewildering fashion. It was a seam bowler's paradise and Gloucester were removed for 153 of which Tom contributed exactly 100. In their second innings they were all out for 107. Once again Tom was the highest scorer with 67, and indeed was very unlucky to be out caught down the leg side off a genuine glance. In this match only two of his colleagues reached double figures, but what was even more impressive was the way he made his runs. Everyone else struggled and failed as the ball moved viciously off the pitch as well as swinging in the air, but Tom never appeared to be in any trouble. It was a classic example of how to bat under really difficult conditions, a triumph of technique and application, which only a great player could produce.

8

PETER MAY

The Amateur with the Professional Approach

One of the tragedies of English cricket, and indeed of cricket throughout the world, was the premature retirement of Peter May. This was driven home to me with renewed force last year when I played with Peter in one of his rare appearances in a Benefit match. On this occasion he happened to be batting alongside some of the best of the current players; he made them look ordinary in comparison, dwarfing them both by execution and presence. He was a great batsman and could still be one. Artists of his calibre are so rare that the game can ill afford to lose them while they are still in their prime.

Peter's departure from the cricket scene as a player was brought about by a combination of business needs, ill-health and domestic circumstances, and, perhaps most important of all, a lessening of interest. In addition he suffered some unfortunate and unhappy experiences during his last two tours abroad.

In 1958–9, Peter May led the M.C.C. to Australia in what was intended, and expected, to be a triumphant tour but, for a wide variety of reasons, it proved a flop. Despite what looked on paper, like a powerful side, England failed abysmally and, as captain, Peter came under a barrage of criticism from the press which might well have worried somebody far more thick-skinned than he was. Even now, at a distance, it is difficult to understand why England played so badly. The throwing controversy certainly did not help, while there was a marked lack of fight on occasions and a tendency for the English party to split into cliques. We had perhaps had rather too much success previously, had lost some of our initial fire and were inclined to be blasé. We were rather like a football side which has known glory, but begins to slide through over-confidence and a declining work rate. What really incensed

Peter, however, was not so much the criticism but the fact that his wife, Virginia, who was then his *fiancée* and also in Australia, was illogically brought into the business. This attack offended Peter's standards of behaviour and left a permanent scar and a distaste for certain sections of the press.

In 1959–60 Peter captained the M.C.C. to unexpected victory in the West Indies in a series dominated by defensive tactics, bouncers, and especially slow over rates. In addition to the strain of commanding the team – I have never found a more conscientious skipper – Peter was troubled by the internal operation he had undergone earlier, and he should never have made the trip. Before the second Test his wound had opened, but despite the considerable pain and great discomfort he kept the matter secret and it was not until the fourth Test that he flew home for urgent medical treatment. I doubt whether any other cricketer would have been prepared to suffer in silence to the same extent.

In these circumstances, it was hardly surprising that he did not make any runs, while differences in outlook between himself and his manager, R. W. V. Robins, could hardly have assisted him to enjoy the tour. When Peter was fully fit once again, and this took a considerable time, he soon came to the conclusion that he had had enough and retired from the game.

I first encountered Peter when I went down with Essex for our annual visit to Fenners. At that time Cambridge University had a number of exceptionally promising players and there were endless arguments as to who would develop into the best batsman – G. H. G. Doggert, J. G. Dewes, D. S. Sheppard, and May himself. On that occasion Peter did not score many runs, but he did strike one fastish good length delivery from me off his back foot past mid-on to the boundary. Then and there I picked him as having the greatest potential, as the ability to play straight bat attacking strokes off the back foot is the hall mark of the class performer. It means that bowlers cannot contain him on a good pitch merely by bowling straight and just short of a length. Subsequently, I was to see him play replicas of this stroke on grounds all over the world, and indeed it became one of the most exciting features of his batting.

Peter made his very impressive *début* for England in 1952 at Leeds against the South Africans and, as I was also a member of the team I had the chance to appreciate its significance at close quarters. He was almost bowled at the very start of his innings, but then proceeded on his way to 138 with a precision, calmness, and certainty which showed very plainly that a new Test star had arrived. It was a knock of remarkable maturity for a person in his very first Test and more than justified the high praise that had been lavished on his batting since he had arrived at Cambridge University. In the following season the Australians, appreciating the danger that May presented to their chances, set about him with their fast bowlers with typical thoroughness. In the first encounter Surrey were caught on a lively pitch and shot out 58 and 122. In the first innings after some superbly hostile bowling by Lindwall – those present claim he has never looked more devastating – Peter went for a duck and only avoided a 'pair' in the second by the narrowest of margins. In the end he only played in two of the Tests, but he went the following winter to the West Indies where he finally squashed any doubts as to his rating as a world class batsman. From that moment, until he retired from the game he was, when fit, an automatic choice for England, and with the departure of Len Hutton, our finest and most reliable player. His one really disappointing series was in South Africa. This was something of a mystery, because outside the Test matches he was in quite exceptional form, indeed I do not think I have ever seen him play better. He reeled off century after century, five coming in his first six first class games. It was not only the runs he made, but the manner in which he executed opposing attacks which was so shattering. Against Rhodesia I shared with him in a stand of 301. It was like batting with a master playing against preparatory schoolboys, yet in ten Test match innings he could only manage an average of 15 and one score of fifty. The fact that Tayfield collected his wicket on four occasions suggested that top-class off-spin might be his Achilles' heel.

On his day Peter May could scatter any attack. I recall one occasion when Essex followed Surrey to Trent Bridge, where Peter had just provided a particularly dazzling exhibition. I asked one of the Nottinghamshire players what his innings had been like: 'It was bloody marvellous. The balls kept coming through the covers like ruddy tracer bullets.' This emphasizes that he was an expert driver both off the front and the back foot. In addition to the splendour of his driving, he was exceptionally strong off his legs, which is so essential in modern cricket. He did not open the face as much as many players and his grip with his right hand was further around the handle than most text books would advocate. Perhaps this is why he was able to punch the ball through the on side so effectively.

Possibly he was occasionally suspect against the off-spinner – and it is certainly true that he did not make as many runs against Glamorgan as against most counties. This was really rather surprising in view of the amount of right hand he put into so many of his shots which normally – Doug Insole was a fine example – indicates a partiality for this type of attack. Because he was tall and weighed considerably more than people imagined, he was never a convincing hooker of really fast bowling. However, he had the height and the ability to play and ride the unpleasant, lifting delivery extremely well, and always appeared to have plenty of time, another sure indication of class. Of course, his defence was excellent, and he kept his nose right over the ball on all occasions. On a difficult wicket, where the ball was apt to pop and stop, he played his dead bat shots with a deliberately angled bat to keep it down. Like all the real experts he also was able to adjust at the very last moment.

I rate Peter very high among the best batsmen I have bowled against. There was not the laughter of Compton in his batting, nor the grace of Hutton, but the authoritative power of his play was very impressive, and I found it extraordinarily difficult to get one past his bat even on a 'green top'.

I played a considerable amount of Test cricket under Peter May and found him a good, very conscientious captain. At times one felt he was almost too conscientious. His captaincy was obviously influenced by his own experiences under Sir Len Hutton and Stuart Surridge with the result that, at his best, he combined some of the drive of Surridge with the tactical tightness of Hutton, although his considerable personal charm tended to cover his hardness on the field. As skipper he demanded dedication and ability and expected loyalty. He was seldom disappointed. Although he never shirked a decision he wisely welcomed suggestions from other players and never hesitated to seek advice. He led and ruled his team, but he was never in any sense an autocrat. By nature and inclination he was not a tactical gambler, so that certainties appealed far more to him than possibilities.

Inevitably captains must expect criticism, as tactics are not automatic and vary from individual to individual. At international level decisions are examined in detail – and the slightest error eagerly pounced upon – even when the mistake only becomes obvious after the event. In the Test match against the West Indies at Edgbaston in 1957 it was suggested afterwards that if Peter had declared earlier, England might have won the match. This was true, but it ignores the fact that if he had declared there was also danger of presenting the game to the opposition after a magnificent rearguard action in which he had played a prominent part. At one time England were 288 runs behind on the first innings, but thanks to a superb stand of 411 by May and Cowdrey, we not only avoided defeat, but were eventually in a position to declare. Nobody has a more vivid recollection of this great rescue act than myself. I happened to be the next man in. I padded up on Saturday evening and Tuesday found me in the same spot, still with my pads on. Those ten hours were among the most tense and tiring I have ever had to endure! In these circumstances he was naturally determined to give the West Indies no chance of regaining the initiative. On a pitch where we had just made 583 for 4, Peter could not afford to dangle the bait of, shall we say, 80 runs per hour before the opposition's powerful, fast scoring batsmen. As things turned out, we could still have won the match if we had held our catches. Four chances were squandered – all difficult – but these make the difference. Certainly no captain can be blamed for his side failing to accept opportunities in the field.

Another time when Peter was unjustifiably accused of being over-cautious was in the fifth Test against the Australians in 1956. On the last day of the rain-affected game, he delayed his declaration until tea. This left the Australians to score 228 in two hours. The fact governing this declaration was not, however, the state of the wicket, but the state of the rubber. England had already recorded two wins to Australia's one, and nothing except an Australian victory could prevent us from retaining the Ashes. Peter decided that he would not give our opponents the slightest chance to escape and share the series by free hitting in a match in which they had been outplayed. If an English victory was the one way we could have won the Ashes, it would have been a different story, and he would have doubtless dangled a very attractive carrot; but a declaration which gave the Australians even the vaguest possibility of success would have been stupid. They had all to gain and nothing to lose. Certainly it was most unlikely that an all-out Australian 'waahoo' would have come off but why present them with the chance? It is amazing how quickly runs can be amassed when everyone swings and fortune favours the brave.

One of the most intriguing features of Peter May's character was the marked difference between the individual and the cricketer. It was almost as if he had two personalities. In normal life he was naturally shy, almost diffident, retiring, introspective and basically rather gentle. I think I have only twice seen him lose his temper and long ago lost count of the many occasions when he had every justification for so doing. He lived according to his own high ethical standards which were intrinsically Edwardian, with Victorian undertones. As a result he was acutely conscious of his responsibilities and his position and tended to worry overmuch about how others would judge his actions. His manners, almost anachronistic in this modern age, were a tribute both to his home and his school. Just as the Nicholas Monserrat character in *The Cruel Sea* was inevitably a Wykehamist, Peter was certainly a Carthusian.

In complete contrast, as a cricketer he always had a hard, almost a ruthless streak. Although he was far too well disciplined to be a bad loser, he was a firm believer in winning. This was hardly surprising when one considers that he started his serious first class career with the powerful Surrey team which felt that winning was almost its right. Although he was an amateur there was nothing light-hearted in the way he played his cricket and he was completely out of sympathy with anyone who allowed extraneous activities to interfere with the job in hand which, for batsmen, was to make runs, for bowlers to take wickets, and for everyone to go flat out in the field. He was certainly far more dedicated to the task of winning than most professionals; he is the amateur with the professional approach.

One of the problems besetting a touring side is the demanding bore. He sidles up to his intended victim, pounces and holds on with all the tenacity of a limpet. Within a matter of moments he has introduced himself, become a life-long friend, and proceeds to discourse at considerable length on a wide variety of subjects, including cricket. How should one deal with this menace? The experienced tourist can normally sense him as he walks into a room and will take immediate action, but even the most cunning and wary are caught from time to time. I always admired the way Peter used to tackle this situation. He was never rude – this method of counter-attack almost inevitably fails – but he would say exactly what was expected and then slide quietly away. However, it was while rooming together in the West Indies that I did discover two May weaknesses. First his singing voice is distinctly short of tone, rhythm and tune. Secondly, he is not invariably courageous. I was awakened in the middle of the night by a strange, unearthly sound. Switching on the light I found to my horror that a bat, the flying variety, was fluttering around the room. As I regard even spiders with distaste, I turned to Peter for comfort and effective help, but to my dismay he had even less appetite for the creature. He immediately took evasive action, disappearing under the safety of the sheets, leaving me to deal with a very nasty situation!

9

COLIN COWDREY

Gentle Knight and Master Batsman

I first met Colin Cowdrey at Scarborough in 1951 when we were both playing for the Gentlemen against the Players. He had played fairly regularly for Kent that summer, and had made an occasional appearance as a seventeen-year-old schoolboy in the previous year, but not against Essex. Naturally I had heard much about him, because he gained a great reputation during his years in the Tonbridge Eleven, which had started when he was only thirteen.

The century Colin scored that day more than justified the glowing accounts. What particularly impressed me was not only the runs, but the way they were made. I had expected to see a schoolboy in action and was amazed at the maturity of this knock. In build as well as technique he reminded me more of a thirty-year-old craftsman than a boy who had captained Tonbridge only a short time before. Quite clearly Colin Cowdrey possessed class. He might and did run into bad patches from time to time, but he was bound to make runs just as surely as January follows December.

For the next two seasons Colin failed to live up to that magnificent innings. Many of the more senior cricketers were sceptical when I enthused over his obvious potential; and it was not until he toured Australia under Sir Len Hutton that he was able to convince everybody that here was not just a good player, but a great one.

I remember a conversation I had in the summer of 1955 with a selector just after the M.C.C. touring party had been announced. He told me – and he was a far better judge of a player than many who have had this job – that it had been touch and go whether Colin or Vic Wilson made the team. I could hardly believe my ears. Although Colin had had a comparatively unproductive season, he possessed the class for which there can never be any substitute, while Vic Wilson could never hope to be more than a useful county cricketer. In the end both players made the trip and my own assessment was upheld.

Curiously enough Cowdrey has, over the years, not made as many runs in county cricket as one might have expected. There have been occasions when I have bowled against him for Essex when he has been almost unrecognizable. He has scratched and pottered around against mediocre bowling, making batting appear an extremely laboured and arduous business. Yet, in form, he is capable of taking apart a powerful international attack. When he is in the mood I always feel that I want to measure his bat, because it seems so much broader than anyone else's, and gives forth an especially melodious sound. For instance, one of the most attractive features of Colin's batting is the way he is able to send the ball skimming through a packed field to the boundary by merely stroking it, such is the delicacy of his touch.

Why is Colin Cowdrey rather more prone to bad patches than most great cricketers? It is certainly not due to any deficiency in technique, because he is admirably correct and always appears to have plenty of time to play his shots. Even against the quickest bowling he does not have to hurry his strokes, which is one of the reasons why the selectors have from time to time tried to convert him into an opener, a position for which he has an almost pathological hatred. Although he has enjoyed a certain amount of success going in first, in the long run it has not assisted his career.

It seems to me that Colin's losses of form are largely the outcome of a character which is rather more complicated than appears on the surface. First and foremost he is a charming person and it is quite inconceivable that anyone should dislike him. He possesses a marked sense of humour and a talent as a mimic which has on many occasions helped to relieve the monotony of a long uneventful stand. Sometimes, even when he is batting, he will do 'a Graveney' – one shoulder higher than the other, the peak-touching routine, and the bat held as if presenting arms. He is also

"Kipper"

ROYULLYETT.

excellent at the Compton waddle-cum-walk and the Laker 'finger' inspection.

Like so many large people he is essentially gentle and decidedly sensitive, while his appetite is almost as prodigious as his capacity for sleep. The former is a guarantee that no hostess will ever be upset by the failure of any team of which Colin is a member to do justice to her cooking. The latter is responsible for his nickname, Kipper, and is a great help to the manager of a touring party because he always knows where to find him, assuming that he is not playing golf, on the beach or writing letters. He is also a confirmed and conscientious worrier. His capacity for worrying when combined with his inborn gentleness and sensitivity is something of a handicap in the tough jungle of professional sport, and has had much to do with those periods when he suddenly descends from being one of the finest batsmen in the world to a struggling county performer. In addition anyone who has a basically sunny disposition must find it hard to apply the intense concentration so essential in all batting for six days per week. Colin has suffered more than most through having to play too much cricket.

It has been said that nobody really enjoys batting against very fast bowling which normally contains a goodly sprinkling of bouncers. I do not entirely subscribe to this but there is certainly more than an element of truth in it. Be that as it may, there is no doubt that Colin was a particularly fine player of pace. One of his secrets was that he would intentionally restrict his backlift at the commencement of an innings. However, Colin has taken a large number of painful blows in Test cricket, especially during the 1959–60 tour in the West Indies when the number of bumpers was particularly high and Colin sported more under-cover protective clothing than an Arctic explorer. However he escaped serious injury until he had his wrist broken by Wes Hall at Lord's in 1963 in one of the most dramatic of all Test matches. This not only kept him out of the game for the remainder of that series but, as so often happens, subconsciously affected his game so that for a considerable period he no longer looked quite as secure against pace as in the past. It was certainly very noticeable in

Jamaica when he faced Hall for the first time after the accident. However, his great tour, the toughest, the 1968 trip to the Caribbean, shows that he has now fully recovered.

At a comparatively early age Colin became captain of Kent but, as until recently his side was short of bowling power, he made rather less impact in terms of results than many inferior leaders who did not suffer this handicap. Colin has a wide knowledge of the game, and is a sound, rather than a spectacular tactician. Before Kent began to make a real impression on the championship, I sometimes felt that Colin was apt to become slightly bored with the proceedings once a match had deteriorated into a dull stalemate, a danger which confronts all captains not blessed with a penetrative and varied attack.

Luck plays a considerable part in captaincy – luck to have the right blend of players, luck to be appointed at the right time, luck to have the complete confidence of those who have made the appointment. As captain of England, Colin has been unfortunate on all three counts. For years he has been the understudy, never the star – a perpetual vice-captain who could be relied upon in an emergency. By nature and upbringing he is very loyal and therefore proved a fine second-in-command. At times I wonder whether his Christian philosophy has not made him prepared to accept situations without complaint that many simply would not have tolerated.

Colin first became captain of England when he took over for the last two Tests in the West Indies from Peter May, who had become ill. He did a solid, unspectacular job carrying out the policies of his predecessor and England returned with the rubber. The next summer he led throughout the whole of a successful series against South Africa, although his own contribution in terms of runs was handicapped by opening the innings. Against both his own inclination and better judgement he allowed himself to be talked into opening instead of using his power to veto. Colin remained in charge for two Tests against the Australians in the following year, but he was still only the caretaker for Peter May, who was put in charge for the last three games. When Peter May retired, the selectors turned to the more flamboyant and controversial Ted Dexter and once again Colin stepped quietly back into the role of vice-captain. Next Mike Smith was appointed to the England captaincy which clearly showed that Colin definitely was not the man the authorities wanted for the job.

Then suddenly and with an illogicality which has been the most outstanding feature of the England selectors for the past decade it was decided to sack Mike Smith after the first Test in 1966 in which he had lost the toss and inevitably the match. This decision sacrificed all the close harmony which he had built up so unassumingly during two overseas tours. The selectors once more turned to Colin Cowdrey and gave him the task of winning the rubber with England already one down. It is doubtful whether any combination would have defeated the West Indies over the series, but things were made even more impossible by the fact that Colin was never entrusted with an even vaguely settled side, indeed only one person, Ken Higgs, was deemed worthy of playing in all five Tests. The outcome was that, after we had been heavily crushed in the fourth Test, the selectors dismissed the unlucky Cowdrey and nobody imagined, including Colin himself, that he would ever skipper England again. However, fate, like England selectors, often moves in mysterious ways. The new England leader, Brian Close, had the full support of the popular press, won a notable victory over Gary Sobers at The Oval, even if the pressure was off, and seemed destined to remain in control for some time to come. Unfortunately Brian allowed a situation in a County match at Edgbaston to cloud his better judgement with the result that the M.C.C., but not, it is interesting to note, the selectors, decided that he was not the person they wanted to lead the M.C.C. in the West Indies. A case could certainly have been made for this on the grounds that Close was not a sufficiently good player at international level, but not on his proven ability as a captain. Be that as it may, the whole sorry affair was both badly and clumsily handled and the selectors were left with the job of finding another skipper. Yet again they resurrected Colin, and this put him in an even more difficult position, not only because he was asked to take over from the person the majority of the country, rightly or wrongly, thought should be in charge, but he was also following a sporting martyr. Because he did such a fine job in the Caribbean and deservedly won the series, even if the eventual outcome hinged on a somewhat unusual declaration, it was suggested that a new Cowdrey had been born. This was not true. Colin remains the same : a dependable, conscientious and slightly defensive leader, but for once fortune was with him. In some respects he is too nice a person, too sensitive and a shade too cautious to be ideal for this much-publicized and criticized position.

His greatest weakness has been his inclination to dither. He has the knowledge, but has sometimes lacked the confidence to make a clear-cut decision, whether it be right or wrong, with the result that the enemy have been occasionally able to wriggle out of what seemed certain defeat. To some extent this is due to his genuine modesty, which makes it difficult for him to appreciate even his own value as a cricketer – I am sure that he does not realize just how well he can bat and I wonder how many times his own team have had to tell him, 'You can do it, skipper' – and this has proved a handicap as captain. A team must have faith in itself, even when it is not entirely justified. This is hard to achieve when the skipper has certain reservations which, because he is an open, honest individual, he cannot easily conceal. Most players have admired Colin as a batsman and liked him as a person, but have sometimes found him lacking in conviction. Absolute honesty may be admirable, but you cannot win at poker and also comply with this moral code.

As Colin has never been very fast over the ground, because of his build, and did not possess an exceptional arm, he soon became a specialist slip. His reactions are excellent, his catching safe, and he is surprisingly agile. I was always delighted to have him in the slips when I was bowling and I also found him a delightful companion when I was stationed alongside. He was ever eager to produce a cheerful aside or a pithy homily. Because he is unspectacular by nature his true ability as a slip fieldsman has not always been fully appreciated.

One of the more interesting and sad features of cricket is the very small number of schoolboy leg-break bowlers who are able to maintain their early promise. The reason for the extremely high casualty rate is that, as they grow, they lose their natural curving flight and often the suppleness of their fingers as well. Colin provides a classic example; at thirteen and fourteen he seemed destined to become a fine leg-spinner, instead of the occasional bowler, much loved by all batsmen, that he is today.

I have seen Colin Cowdrey play many outstanding innings in various parts of the world, but the most memorable was, perhaps, the century he made in Melbourne in the vital third Test of 1954–5 which enabled us to win that match. Colin went to the crease with the score at 21 for 2, Lindwall and Miller in full cry, and, as is so often the case on the first morning of a match, a Melbourne pitch which was full of life. I joined him at 41 for 4 and was fascinated by the way he dealt with some fine hostile bowling. His defensive technique was perfect, yet he kept the score moving with a series of drives off both the front and the back foot, while he also forced the ball off his legs with great skill. He went on to make 102 out of 191, an innings of character, charm and enormous value.

I have always been fond of batting with Colin. First, because I have complete faith in his judgement of what safely constitutes a run. He is faster between the wickets than his bulk might suggest and he loves to pinch singles. Second, he can make batting appear not quite the impossible task it so often seems to be. Third, he loves a chat between overs which helps to relieve the tension when things are hard.

Personally, I shall always be indebted to him, not only for the pleasure of playing with and against him but because his presence has invariably helped to make the game itself all the more enjoyable. In consequence I was sickened when I learned of the treatment he received after the England defeat at Leeds in 1966 by the West Indies. Those who were responsible for scratching his car and letting down his tyres one can dismiss as wanton hooligans, but it is hard to forgive the West Indian player who contemptuously ignored him, after he had taken the trouble to go to their dressing room and congratulate the side, both individually and collectively, on having won the series. Chivalry may be dead, but one likes to believe that common courtesy is not also extinct.

10

KEN BARRINGTON

The Accumulator

Ken Barrington has already played in over seventy Test matches and has scored more than 6,000 runs, including eighteen centuries and thirty-three fifties. These figures have already established him in the record books; but as Barrington is still in his prime there is every reason to suppose that, before he retires, his run-gathering will be even more phenomenal; his eventual aggregate could well exceed all others.

At the moment he is one of the few automatic choices for England, a master batsman of world class, yet he does not possess the same box-office appeal as a number of players of considerably less ability. There are a number of reasons for this, some of which are not really connected with the game itself. For example, Ken has an average appearance and lacks distinctive characteristics. He is not tall and willowy, he is not small and neat, he is not a superb mover and he does not possess eye-catching blond hair. He is of medium height, somewhat stockily built with features of considerable strength which have been hewn rather than delicately chiselled. He has an inbred cautious streak, so that there has never been the slightest risk of his developing into a compulsive spender, or finishing in the bankruptcy court! One can imagine him as a sound, dependable yeoman rather than a knight in shining armour and his weapons are more likely to be the broad sword or the cudgel rather than the rapier. This ordinariness and lack of colour are reflected in his batsmanship which, although I admire it enormously, fails to excite me in the same way as that of Compton, or Kanhai or Neil Harvey. This has nothing to do with the fact that he sometimes gathers his runs slowly. Throughout his Test career he has probably scored consistently faster than

Hanif Mohammed, but I prefer to watch the little master from Pakistan.

Why does Ken's batting affect me this way? I believe that the cause is tied up with his unusual and highly individual technique which he has evolved over the years. Although it is admirably sound, and undoubtedly effective, it is aesthetically rather ugly; like the music-hall mother-in-law who is not pretty to look at and usually stays a long time. Obviously, I much prefer, from the playing angle, a player who makes runs irrespective of his style, rather than a man who looks good, but seldom does; yet at the highest level I have always expected the odd touch of uninhibited genius to break through from time to time. Ken has disciplined himself to such a degree that this happens on fewer occasions (when he is at the crease) than with any other great cricketer I have encountered – and there is no disputing that he is in the highest class. He has made run-gathering his business, and a highly profitable one, so that at times he reminds me of a computer, admirably efficient, but a shade lacking in soul.

However, this does not mean there is not much to regard with pleasure in the Barrington technique, quite the reverse. I have bowled against him when runs flowed from his bat as they did so delightfully in the first Test match against Pakistan in the summer of 1967. This was a memorable, chanceless innings, chockfull of powerful strokes, and clearly displaying the authority of the star performer. I have bowled against him when conditions were difficult and runs hard to come by, and he has coped with the situation with comfort. I have bowled against him when he has been out of form, but equally determined not to surrender his wicket easily. This last is one of the most significant features of his play. He seldom returns to the pavilion as a result of an ill-judged shot; he nearly always has to be got out!

As a bowler I have always been particularly impressed by the way he is able to 'ride' a lifting delivery and drop it dead. He also has the ability to adjust his stroke at the last moment when the ball has moved off the pitch.

There is a myth that English batsmen are vulnerable against wrist-spinners, although figures in international cricket since the

Ken Barrington
A Music Hall
Mother-in-Law
style of battin.
Not beautif
to look at
and mostl
stays a
long tim

war do not support the theory. In fact, a large number thrive on this particular form of attack, despite the present scarcity in county cricket; while both Yorkshire and Surrey at their peak have been able to win the County Championship without one. Ken Barrington is particularly partial to leg-break bowling despite the fact that he seldom finds it necessary to advance down the pitch. He is content to play it safely from the confines of the crease with the deadest of dead bats, and to despatch the inevitable bad delivery with precision to the boundary. He is helped in this by his ability to read the googly.

There are two failings in Barrington's batting which both stem directly from his desire to sell his wicket dearly. First, for a player of his stature he seldom assumes complete control of a situation or systematically destroys an attack. Secondly, he has a tendency, in his pursuit of more runs, to overlook the practical considerations of a particular contest. A few years ago Essex were playing Surrey. At lunchtime on the third day Surrey had a handsome lead on a reliable pitch. Their only real chance of victory lay in an early declaration and the hope that they would bowl us out while we were trying to chase a large total against the clock. Essex went out after the interval and I employed two spinners, Robin Hobbs and Paddy Phelan. Surrey had only lost two second innings wickets and Barrington was one of the not-out batsmen. This was the obvious time for quick runs as wickets simply did not matter, but Ken has never fancied himself as a sacrificial lamb. Even so, I was mystified when my two spinners were allowed to operate with normal field placings for some forty-five minutes without a shot in anger being played against them. Barry Knight, who was taking life easily in the covers, asked what the devil was going on. It was an incomprehensible piece of cricket and meant that Mickey Stewart had to delay his declaration which in turn cost Surrey the match. If his batsmen had only given his bowlers another half-hour, as they should have done, they must have won comfortably.

Ken has been accused of batting too slowly and the instance just quoted was an example, but there have also been occasions when he has been condemned unfairly. The most notorious case was probably the Edgbaston Test against the New Zealanders in 1965. Our selectors decided to overlook the fact that at the time Ken was in the middle of probably the worst patch in his career; or possibly they did not realize it, though it was patently obvious to everyone else. Alternatively, it might be argued that they were banking on class. However, when a player is so blatantly, though temporarily, out of touch it is surely unnecessary to chance him in a Test match at home, against unspectacular opposition, when there are normally plenty of bats available who are in the runs. It so happened I played against Ken in a Benefit match on the Sunday immediately preceding this Test. I was bowling when Ken, desperately short of runs and confidence, came to the wicket. Although it was a limited overs contest, and I was operating at little above medium pace, Ken batted as if I were Alec Bedser in his prime. He was so out of touch that he did not look a good club player, let alone an international. When Ken went in to bat at Edgbaston against a steady, accurate seam attack supported by a well stationed field, his reaction was entirely predictable. He decided to graft for his runs, which he acquired slowly and painfully until he had the satisfaction of reaching a laboured century. It was, in its way, a remarkable feat. The selectors' reaction was to discipline him publicly, for unenterprising batting without his captain or anyone else, as far as I know, forcibly indicating their displeasure during any of the many intervals that were available. I have always thought that the real culprits in this unfortunate affair were those who chose someone who was so out of touch rather than Barrington himself. To make it even more illogical, in 1967 Ken produced an even more gruesome grind against Pakistan at Trent Bridge, but on this occasion the selectors decided to overlook his slowness, which obviously had the approval of his captain, Brian Close, and undoubtedly helped England to achieve an easy victory.

Ken Barrington was a very junior member of the all-conquering Surrey combination when I first met him, and I was immediately impressed by his potential. In those days he had a normal stance, a considerable range of fluent strokes, including a spectacular square cut which sometimes despatched the short ball to the boundary over cover's head, and a sound defence. What finally convinced me that here was a player of exceptional ability was when he joined in a lengthy partnership with Peter May, who was currently the finest player in the land, and probably in the world. I, in company with the other toiling bowlers, was hammered impressively to all quarters of the ground and young Ken was by no means overshadowed by the genius of his partner. When I tried to contain him by bowling just short of a length, Ken drove off his back foot through the reinforced covers in a way which certainly did not suffer in comparison with Peter who was a wonderful exponent of this particular shot.

Ken caught the eye of the selectors and he was picked to play against South Africa in 1955 before, possibly, he was quite ready. The outcome was that he lost his place and then, as so often has happened, was illogically forgotten. It was during this period as a 'didn't quite make it' that Ken began a systematic and methodical tightening-up of his game. He adopted an exaggerated two-eyed or, to be more accurate, two-shouldered stance, ruthlessly eliminated the more flamboyant and dangerous of his shots, reinforced his defence, and gradually became one of the most consistent acquirers of runs in the land. If runs were needed to establish oneself permanently in the England team, runs they should have. It should also be remembered that, quite apart from the honour, hardly any cricketers who fail to become regular internationals have much hope of making money out of the game.

Ken's initial batting movement is back and across and this gives him more time against fast bowling. When he decides to play forward, his front leg cannot reach as far down the pitch as a forward mover and to counter this disadvantage, his right leg shuffles over behind his bat and provides an additional barrier. This is an effective rather than an attractive defensive ploy and if it becomes an automatic reaction, as it has in Ken's case, it tends to hinder the cover drive. In addition, Ken's two-shouldered stance also makes off side driving more difficult, because the left foot has such a long way to go before it is in the correct position; but, on the profit side, it has helped with his on-side shots. He is an artist at nudging the ball away off his legs for ones and twos.

In an era of tight defensive cricket, the value of this cannot be over-emphasized. The initial move back, combined with his very open stance, has also helped him with his hooking and pulling. Unless it is *very* fast, Ken relishes short bowling, as in addition to his hooking and pulling he is exceptionally proficient at the cut.

When Ken was eventually recalled to the Test scene he was an infinitely more mature player and he set about the task of gathering runs with unsurpassed dedication. In the 1959–60 Caribbean tour he withstood the West Indian fast bowlers with considerable courage. Bouncers were frequent so that he received more than his fair share of unpleasant knocks. During his two trips to Australia his stature increased and on both occasions he was England's most successful batsman while his hundred in the fifth Test at Melbourne was the quickest of the series and made nonsense out of those critics who claimed he was short of shots. His tour of South Africa was another triumph. Almost inevitably he scored more runs than anyone else and averaged over 100 in the Test series.

It is interesting how Ken has dominated the English batting to a much greater extent abroad than he has done at home. With less continuous cricket and no county commitments, he has been able to concentrate on the job in hand and the results have been remarkable both in terms of runs and consistency. However, it was probably on the easy-paced and placid pitches of India and Pakistan that his solid defence, professional approach, concentration and thirst for runs paid their biggest dividends. Once he had settled it seldom appeared even possible for him to lose his wicket. One big innings followed another. Nothing seemed to worry him, least of all the opposing bowlers.

Ken is a dependable fieldsman, rather than a brilliant one, and has a good pair of hands. He is also an interesting bowler, who has perhaps never realized his full potential. To bowl a leg-break well, it is necessary to have plenty of practice in the middle. He can bowl a dangerous leg-break, a presentable googly, and a fair top-spinner, but there is an understandable tendency for him to stray off line. He certainly enjoys his bowling and his gestures of frustration, when he beats the bat and fails to induce the desired result, show the influence of his former colleague, Tony Lock. His batting is very undemonstrative, but when bowling he is prepared to give full range to his emotions. His action is not pretty, but his arm comes over quickly and he does make the odd delivery hurry through and bounce. I have always been pleased to see him come on when I have been batting, even though he has trapped me from time to time with a long hop! However, comparatively speaking and like all bowlers of his kind, he is more formidable abroad where he frequently troubles the opposition with his bounce and break. This is especially true in the minor up-country matches when the inexperienced opposition is often reasonably secure against seam, but utterly bemused and baffled by wrist-spin.

Until he knows you, Ken Barrington is inclined to be diffident. In his early days he was unsure of himself and has never fully recovered from the shock of finding himself an international expert and not merely another inhabitant of London. One gains the impression that he would make a good neighbour, quiet, reliable and always prepared to offer advice. This last characteristic often has its humorous side – take him for a drive in your brand new car and within seconds he will have heard an ominous rattle and be under the bonnet tracing the source, with rather more enthusiasm than technical know-how. But he is also decidedly sensitive and takes things rather more intensely than many people appreciate. In 1967 he suffered a minor breakdown, which entailed a complete rest from the game. He had found the strain of an exhausting but very remunerative Benefit, coming on top of years of hard competitive international cricket, too much. Now he has fully recovered and also rediscovered his insatiable hunger for runs. He will score many more centuries for England before he decides to retire.

D

II

E. R. DEXTER

'Lord Edward'

I have always felt that 'Lord Edward' was born several genera-
tions too late : he would have fitted naturally into the times when
the English aristocracy possessed real power. Although Ted is not
an aristocrat, tall and handsome he looks the part or, to be more
accurate, he looks like what people expect a lord to be, while he
certainly plays cricket in the grand manner. It is easy to imagine
him riding recklessly to hounds, fighting a somewhat disdainful
duel, or gracefully adorning the more spectacular royal revelries.
If he had lived in Hollywood he must surely have been in constant
demand whenever it was decided to produce another historical
epic about England. He would have made a splendid Essex or
Buckingham in celluloid.

Ted is one of that rare breed who have been given an outstanding physique – over six feet, powerfully yet gracefully built – and
also a natural aptitude for all games. He is a very fine golfer and
possessed the ability to be an outstanding Rugby player. One golf
enthusiast, who had just seen Ted eat up a course with an ease
and distinction that would have pleased a tournament professional,
lamented that he had not concentrated on the game. He certainly
could have become an amateur international golfer, although I
doubt whether he would have ever mustered the singleness of purpose and absolute dedication necessary to win the big tourna-
ments and the big money. Ted would have found difficulty in
making any game the motivating force in his life. He was one of
those players whose potential normally exceeded his execution.

I first encountered Ted in the summer of 1956 when Essex
had their annual fixture with Cambridge University. The University were dismissed somewhat cheaply and, although Ted's
own contribution was modest, it was easy to see that a player of

distinction and colourfulness had arrived. Nothing could disguise the authoritative ring of his bat, the high backlift with the full follow-through, nor his build and swashbuckling appearance. I was especially impressed by his driving off his back foot which was easily the most decisive I had seen from a University player since Peter May. It was too early to decide on his quality, but here was a natural entertainer, someone who had crowd appeal, and I merely wished that he had been born in Essex. In the following year a not-out century of power and charm seldom produced by an undergraduate dispersed all doubts. Here was a top-class batsman plainly destined for Test cricket. It was merely a question of time. When I was unable to play in the fourth Test at Leeds, Ted was invited to join the twelve, but an injury forced him to decline.

Gossip flows freely in County cricket and I heard on the grapeline that Ted, who was captaining Cambridge in 1958, was one of the more theory-conscious of performers. There was nothing unusual about that as, if one does not think or experiment or inquire while an undergraduate, one probably never will. However, apart from holding some unusual ideas Ted was also a practical theorist, as he showed when Essex met the University at Brentwood. Ted was in the thirties and, if not quite at the top of his form, nevertheless looked both secure and impressive. A Cambridge wicket fell and, while the new batsman was taking a fairly leisurely stroll to the wicket, he explained to me that he was not entirely satisfied with his present grip, which, I might add, had already brought him a considerable number of runs that season. He was therefore experimenting with a new one. I have favoured adjustments in the nets, or in unimportant matches, but never in a first class game, however, I was impressed by the obvious confidence in his own ability which enabled him to do this effectively against a County attack.

Ted's views and outlook on the game as a whole were also interesting and often refreshingly different. One could not help admiring his obvious conviction even when disagreeing with him. Like all young reformers he was a shade intolerant and had little time for another point of view.

"Lord" Ted
Out of his time.

The following winter I went on that tour to Australia under Peter May, when we were unceremoniously knocked off our perch as unofficial cricket champions of the world. There were many who felt that Ted should have been chosen, including a large section of the press, always quick to appreciate a player with an obvious talent for making runs and news. However, he was not selected and our party from the outset was hit by injuries. Willie Watson hurt himself on the slip and had to undergo an operation in Australia, Subba Row fractured a wrist, and after the first Test my effectiveness as a bowler was reduced because I was unable to put my left foot down firmly, owing to a back injury which did not mend until I underwent a manipulative operation the following summer. These were but three of the setbacks we encountered and it was therefore decided to send for reinforcements in the shape of Ted Dexter and John Mortimore.

Ted's arrival was entirely in keeping with the image he was acquiring, the aristocratic playboy. At the time he was working in Paris which, by itself was worth half a paragraph. Although English cricketers have a wide variety of winter jobs, additional members for overseas touring teams do not normally have to be extracted from the French capital. I shall always treasure my first glimpse of him in Australia, elegantly and gaily clad, looking like one of those male models in one of the more exclusive colour magazines, conservatively trendy, or what the young man-about-town sports in his leisure moments! All that was now required was a stimulating century and he would have won Australia which has an amusing and somewhat touching regard for the English aristocracy, perhaps because they have none of their own. Unfortunately, but understandably, Ted was unable to live up to his image on the field. The transformation was too quick, experience had yet to come, and perhaps he was too ambitious. He also had the disadvantage of joining a party which was in the process of disintegration and rapidly completing its own downfall by splitting into groups. As a result there was nobody who said 'this is no picnic, get your bloody head down, Ted'. As it was nothing went right for him. He was chosen for the third Test on promise, got off the mark, and then, plainly bewildered by an attacking field which suggested Laker on an Oval turner and not Slater on a good track, allowed himself to be bowled for one. Still patently out of form, he played in the fifth Test but was able to contribute little. His bowling, which had always tended to be unpredictable made even less impression in Australia. To be suddenly cast in the deep end of an Australian series out of practice and out of touch was enough to have upset a far more mature player but what was disappointing was that it even affected Ted's fielding. With his natural athleticism, eye for a moving ball and quick reactions, Ted had been regarded as a brilliant, though sometimes erratic fieldsman, but in Australia he was merely erratic, his returns proving especially hazardous for all except the batsmen.

In retrospect, this lack of success was probably fortunate because it made Ted realize that cricket at international level was very different from the sub-standard first class game encountered at the university. In his first full season with Sussex he often batted brilliantly, but with more circumspection, so that when he was invited to tour the West Indies the following winter he was able to make the transition from a dashing apprentice into a batsman of Test proportions with an aggregate of over 500 runs for the series. Nothing was more impressive than the way he handled the short, fast bowling of which there was an over-abundance. His own height, upright stance, and complete lack of fear all helped. From that moment, until his premature retirement, Ted remained an automatic selection for England as well as one of the leading box-office attractions. He was a controversial character and an exciting batsman, the ideal mixture. In full flow it was not too much to claim that he was worth at least double the admission price. Relatively speaking, he was more impressive for England than for Sussex, although at both levels I always felt he would have made more runs with more self-discipline, but of course, if he had done this, he would not have been Dexter. The overall aggregate would have been increased, but the colour would have diminished.

When Essex met Sussex my tactics against Ted were straightforward and often paid. If we were unable to dismiss him in the first fifteen minutes, I would set a defensive field and try to make the safe scoring of runs a lengthy business. Faced by this in a County match Ted had the utmost difficulty in not accepting the challenge and so taking the risks it entailed. Occasionally the result would be an adventurous century, but the odds were very much in my favour so that his average against Essex was small for a player of his calibre, as indeed it was throughout his career in County cricket. Quite apart from his impetuosity and his disinclination to be constrained by opposing bowlers, Ted found the six-day routine of domestic competition apt to become a bore. His downfall was more often the result of his own temperament than the skill of opposing bowlers.

Although Ted was at times regarded as an all-rounder I felt that he was too much of an enigma as a bowler to justify that rating. He could bowl extremely well, but his line and length were always liable to become wayward. The reason was probably that he never practised sufficiently for his action to become grooved, so that he could not be relied upon to shut up an end for an afternoon, something which the third seamer in a Test team must be prepared to undertake from time to time. He really was a world-class batsman who could turn his arm over, sometimes to great effect. At his best he was a lively attacking fast-medium who moved the ball in the air, was a shade quicker than he appeared, and was always experimenting. Certainly Gordon Barker, reliable and professional opening bat for Essex, used to rate him very highly among new ball bowlers but, although Ted was capable of producing highly unpleasant deliveries, he was seldom able to maintain for long periods the nagging accuracy of the English seamer who can be relied upon to pick up a hundred wickets per year. His bowling reminded me of a whirlwind, potentially destructive and quite unpredictable.

As a player for England Ted did everything that was required and often more, but as captain he was not always as good as he might have been if he had had to wait a little longer for the appointment. Perhaps, even more important, if this had been the case he would have remained longer in the game instead of retiring early, having tasted all the honours. Ted was only twenty-six when he was made skipper of England and in certain respects was decidedly naïve. In particular it seemed to me that he had difficulty in really understanding some players whose outlook and background were so very different from his own. This might not have mattered in the amateur thirties, but was something of a handicap in the democratic and professional sixties. On occasions he gave the impression that he was incapable of being *sympathique,* not because he was by intention or desire unfeeling, but merely because the other person's reaction never occurred to him. This was not helped by Ted himself being a far more complex individual than is often realized, and there is a tendency for people to regard with suspicion anything or anybody that they cannot comprehend. Some were further misled by his self-sufficiency and his self-conviction, while his manner could appear a shade remote and even autocratic. In fact underneath there dwells an individual who is shy, generous, romantic, remarkably catholic in his tastes, and with a sentimental streak which is very far removed from the somewhat egocentric picture that is often regarded as his true image.

As a tactician Ted was sound and realistic; although he liked gay cricket he was willing to play it as tight as anyone if he felt that that would help his overall plan. He showed this when he relied largely on a non-stop diet of seam when playing for Sussex, and when, after centuries by Bill Lawry in two Tests he decided to contain the Australian, then a non-cutter, by instructing his bowlers to direct their attack just short of a length, outside the off stump. This did not stop Lawry scoring but reduced his tempo to a leisurely amble. Perhaps Ted's biggest weakness as a captain was that when he made a mistake it took him a long time to realize it. In Australia he attempted to tell David Allen, a tried and experienced campaigner, how and where to bowl. If a mature cricketer does not know what is the most effective method for disposing of batsmen by the time he is playing in Test cricket he should not have been chosen in the first place. Advise, encourage and occasionally rebuke, but it seldom pays to instruct players on the intricacies of their chosen craft. They will almost certainly resent it – I should have done – and tends to destroy the harmony between captain and bowler which ought to exist.

Another example of Ted's considerable tactical grasp of cricket was the way that Sussex twice carried off the Gillette Cup under his command. He quickly appreciated that a slightly different approach was needed for limited-over cricket and that a team like Sussex with a number of good stroke players and accurate seam bowlers was ideally equipped for it. His effective defensive deployments in the field may have brought some caustic comments, but they also brought the trophy back to Hove.

Whenever I think of Ted Dexter batting two occasions stand out. The first was in the second Test at Lord's against the West Indies in 1963. Once again the English openers had both failed, Charlie Griffith having claimed the wickets of Stewart and Edrich for two and nought, and a collapse seemed imminent. In this tense and dangerous situation Ted played one of his most courageous, spectacular and valuable innings. He met the pace and the hostility of Griffith and Hall with equal ferocity, carving them to all parts of Lord's with a series of eye-dazzling drives, cuts and hooks. His fifty came in under fifty minutes (and neither Wes nor Charlie complete their overs quickly). Eventually he fell lbw to Sobers for 70 scored at a run a minute. It not only transformed the game, but set Lord's alight in a way that caused the more aged to recall Gilbert Jessop, and made everyone present realize what a tremendously exciting spectacle cricket can be.

The second occasion was when Ted and I went on a short tour of Jamaica sponsored by Carreras. In addition to it proving a delightful and happy trip, Ted produced a couple of centuries of a brilliance which few could have equalled and none surpassed. He reached one hundred in sixty-four minutes without slogging. He merely played his shots but hit them with more brutality than I had witnessed for a very long time. The fast, the medium, and the slow bowlers were all treated with what almost amounted to regal disdain and their best deliveries were sent violently careering to the boundary while quite a number finished outside Sabina Park. Ted received one good-length ball from Rudy Cohen, a tall, lively fast bowler which he drove on the up off his front foot. It very nearly took Cohen with it, soared over the sight screen, and, still on the rise was last seen disappearing into the outskirts of Kingston. It was a *tour de force*, and accentuated his loss to the game, especially when one realizes that he may well have never reached his zenith.

I joined Ted when he was in the nineties of his other hundred and he came up to me and very nicely, but rather unnecessarily suggested that I ought not to hit the ball too hard as it was rather like a stone. I pushed gingerly forward, took my single, and never did find out the hardness of that particular ball, as Ted solved the problem typically by sweeping Alf Valentine well clear of the ground from whence it was never recovered.

12

ROHAN KANHAI
The Magician from Guyana

Rohan Kanhai is not the greatest batsman I have bowled against but few, if any, have had the power to fascinate and satisfy me more. Just as the sauces can transform a good meal into a feast, it is the stroke execution that garnishes a Kanhai innings which would make it unforgettable even when his score is not particularly large.

Rohan Kanhai is a Guyanan of Indian extraction and like the most exciting cricketers of Asian origin there is more than a touch of eastern magic about his batting. For, though slightly and almost delicately built, he has overcome this by a combination of timing, eye and the use of his wrists. He has the ability to flick, almost caress the ball to the boundary, which is especially attractive. On one occasion I fractionally overpitched a ball on his off stump. He drove it and at the very last moment impacted an extra touch of right hand, slightly angled the bat so that it streaked between mid-wicket and mid-on before either could move.

Always assuming that I am not the recipient, I love to see a towering six from someone like Sobers or Dexter, but because they are both big and strong it does not have quite the same appeal as one by Rohan who appears not to have the necessary physique to strike the ball either as far or as hard. I remember one remarkable blow by him at Edgbaston, for the Rest of the World against an England XI, which had to be seen to be believed. In the first innings the English seamers had dismissed the World side for a comparatively small score on a pitch where the ball moved about considerably, but it dried out into a fine wicket for their second innings. Tom Cartwright – who tends to be underrated because he is unspectacular in method, but is, especially in English conditions, an artist – was keeping his usual immaculate length. He

Rohan Kanhai

sent down a good delivery on or about the leg stump to Rohan, who picked it up on the rise and deposited it over the top of the long on stand. It was a wonderful example of his ingenuity and also of the power with which so slight a man can hit.

Rohan naturally possesses a wide range of strokes some of which are completely original. He has become especially famous for a cross between a pull and a sweep which he attempts to lash so fiercely that he ends up flat on his back. Although this is spectacular, from the purely technical angle it might be termed an extravagance, but then Rohan is essentially an extravagant and colourful performer. He is always liable to embark upon strokes which others would not consider, let alone attempt to execute. This flamboyant approach to batting has on many occasions brought about his downfall, but is the reason why I find him so satisfying. When he is at his very best there is more than a touch of genius about his play which has an aesthetic appeal. He reminds me of a great athletic conjurer whose tricks sometimes fail – not because of inability, but because he attempts so much, sometimes even the impossible – he is seldom mundane. If I could choose how I would like to be able to bat, I would select Kanhai as my model. Perhaps the reason is the same for the many comedians who want to play Hamlet!

One stroke in the Kanhai repertoire that appeals especially to my taste is his slash off the front foot, struck on the up, which sends the ball skimming through the covers. He tends to play this shot a shade later than most, thus making it even more difficult for a fieldsman to intercept.

Because Rohan is one of the finest, as well as one of the most exhilarating cricketers of his generation, he has in addition to his vast range of attacking shots a basically sound defensive technique which will become of ever-increasing value as age gradually reduces the keenness of his eye and his swiftness of movement. Inevitably his play is becoming more conservative and less flamboyant. At one time his impetuosity – which in his early days as international ace he was able to ignore because his reactions were so fast that he still scored consistently – threatened to end his Test career earlier than was necessary. When the M.C.C. went to the

West Indies in 1968 many people believed that Rohan was almost finished at this level and certainly his batting in the two previous West Indian tours to England had failed to come up to his full potential. However, the English bowlers found a Kanhai who had realized, before it was too late, that he had started to slip and was prepared to make the necessary amendments to both his technique and his temperament. He became an altogether more determined, more conscientious performer, and scored over 500 runs in the series. In the past he has often been somewhat irresponsible both on and off the field, but now he has disciplined himself to a degree which has surprised many who had written him off as past his peak. To my mind this represents a bigger victory over himself than over cricket, as his failures were more due to his own personality than to any basic deficiency in his method.

The automatic reaction of most fast bowlers when they find themselves confronted by a small, comparatively slight Indian who is quick on his feet – and is able to deal competently and often demoralizingly with the spinners – is to start a blasting operation. Sometimes those tactics have proved effective, but not against Rohan Kanhai who was brought up in a school where it was essential to conquer physical fear of flying bouncers in order to reach the top. He has the ability and courage to hook Wesley Hall at his fastest, while he also possesses what the services might term the moral fibre or 'guts' to accept philosophically the inevitable knocks that will occur when facing pace bowling on a nasty track. Although he scored over 500 runs in the 1968 series against the M.C.C., including two centuries, it is doubtful whether anything impressed Colin Cowdrey and his side more than the way he withstood the barrage of speed in the West Indies' first innings at Sabina Park, when the ball was behaving so unpredictably. His technique in stopping the shooter and the impassive way he accepted the physical battering was an exhibition of improvisation, skill and considerable courage.

I first encountered Rohan Kanhai when he came to this country for the first time in 1957 under John Goddard. Although there was a wealth of talent among the players in the party, they failed to do themselves justice, were somewhat lacking in harmony, and were heavily defeated in the Tests. Rohan was originally chosen as a reserve wicket-keeper-cum-batsman, and, although he was not as efficient behind the stumps as Gerry Alexander, he kept wicket in the first three Tests because of his obvious superiority with the bat. In the fourth and the fifth Tests Rohan was chosen purely for his batting and at the end of the trip he wisely decided to concentrate on developing his greatest asset. As a keeper, like Clyde Walcott before him, he was never more than adequate and this is not sufficient at the highest level, especially in England where the bounce and the movement of the ball is so much more pronounced than in the Caribbean.

Rohan's decision to hang up his gloves gave the West Indies another fine all-round fieldsman. In the deep his fleetness of foot, mobility and accurate throwing make him a menace to all batsmen, especially if they are foolish enough to attempt a risky single. Bearing this in mind and his often uncanny skill with the bat, I often regretted he never played hockey. Surely he possessed all the pre-requisites to excel at this game.

As is so often the case with those who have had considerable experience behind the stumps, Rohan was also a fine slip fielder. However, on a hot day and with the opposition plodding comfortably along to a large total, his concentration was liable to flag and then his temperament was better suited to the more active demands of fielding in the deep.

If Rohan failed to impress to any marked degree behind the stumps, it was a very different matter when he was at the crease. Here quite patently was a cricketer of exceptional talent. On his first tour the West Indies were unable to find a satisfactory opening partnership and Rohan was pressed into service for the first and second Tests. Obviously this was not his ideal position, and since he was also being called upon to keep wicket, it was plainly asking too much of an inexperienced, young cricketer who had had no previous experience of English wickets. In the remaining three Tests his position in the order varied so that he never had the satisfaction of a settled niche. One felt that the West Indies knew they possessed an expert in the art of attack demolition, but were unable to make up their minds how best to employ him. He did not make a big score in this series, but the forties he produced suggested that, with time and a curbing of his natural impetuosity, he would rectify this in the years ahead. It seemed to me then that perhaps the younger members of this West Indian side were not receiving all the help, advice and encouragement that they might have expected from their seniors.

It was not until the West Indies toured India and Pakistan that Rohan developed into a world class player. He then scored more runs than anyone against both countries, including double centuries which plainly indicated that he possessed the mental application necessary for the really large innings, and that he was certainly more than a dashing stroke-maker. He was not so effective or so brilliant in the rather dull series against England in the Caribbean in 1959–60, but any doubts as to whether the perfect pitches in Asia had led to his being overrated were dispelled once and for all when he went with Sir Frank Worrell's team to Australia in 1960–1. He was the player who first caught the imagination of the Australian public with a flowing century against an Australian XI at the start of the tour and followed this up with a breath-taking double century on his initial appearance in Melbourne. In the Tests he had the highest aggregate as well as the distinction of scoring a century in each innings at Adelaide. This was perhaps the zenith of his career for, until a new Kanhai emerged in 1968 in the West Indies, there was a gradual but definite decline in his batting prowess. He occasionally produced innings of genius, but these were liable to be interspersed with too many periods of comparative mediocrity. When he made his second trip to England in 1963 under Sir Frank Worrell, he averaged over 55 with the highest aggregate of 497 runs, but he never made a century and lost his wicket too often through an indiscretion when well set and when a large score should have been forthcoming. This slide from being one of the finest batsmen in the world to just a very good Test cricketer was even more marked on his third tour to England in 1966 when he had to wait until the fifth Test for a century which took nearly four hours and strangely enough was his only one in this country.

In the League Rohan made a large number of runs, but

frequently gave the impression that he should have done better. He was never of the dominating force of, for instance, Everton Weekes. In the same way as a great actor experiences difficulty in raising his performance in a small suburban theatre, Rohan frequently found that this type of cricket failed to stimulate him, with the result that he was inclined to produce the flashy stroke in an effort to be spectacular. The gap between what is batting genius and what is dashing recklessness can be very narrow. Cut a good length ball off the stumps for four and everyone applauds rapturously. Play the same shot and be bowled and one is automatically condemned. This is best summed up in that classically useless instruction to batsmen, much loved by T. N. Pearce, 'Play your shots but don't get out'.

Rohan fought his way to the top through ability and with remarkably little coaching, yet it is interesting to note how correct is his basic technique. Because he is intelligent with a natural instinct for the game, he soon realized that, to make the type of runs necessary to be considered for first class cricket, it paid to employ a straight bat for defensive strokes as well as for many of the attacking ones. His prowess as a cricketer eventually provided him with a reasonable and, by Caribbean standards, very good standard of living. It also enabled him to see the world and spend a good deal of time playing the sport he loved so much. In his early days he was inclined to be suspicious of people, Anglo-Saxons in particular, which stemmed from his background and from being a little unsure of himself. He had moved into a world which was in many ways different from the one in which he had been reared and some of the differences confused, amused and occasionally angered him. He has always been sensitive so that he was liable to think that he had been slighted, and to take offence even when none was intended. He was apt also to brood over a wrong, imagined or otherwise, for far longer than would a West Indian of African extraction. At one time I gained the impression that he had something of a 'chip on his shoulder' and that this occasionally led to clashes with authority which could easily have been avoided. The flashes of impetuosity and rashness in his batting are also part of his character, and his character, like his batting, can sparkle or simmer.

I did not know Rohan Kanhai well until I managed the Rothman World and West Indian sides. Until then he had been to me a very fine, somewhat unpredictable cricketer. However living and talking with him, I began to understand what he thought and why. I liked what I found and now admire the man underneath as well as the cricketer. He is an engaging companion who has mellowed with the years, and I shall always treasure the glory of his stroke play. Now that he has joined Warwickshire lovers of the game will have many opportunities to see this great entertainer in action. In the years that lie ahead he will doubtless add much in terms of both gaiety and runs to our domestic scene.

13

RAY LINDWALL

The Complete Fast Bowler

Fast bowlers are always more formidable when they can hunt in pairs, Gregory and McDonald, Larwood and Voce, Trueman and Statham, Hall and Griffith, Heine and Adcock, Lindwall and Miller. This makes certain that the unfortunate batsman cannot escape to peace and quiet at the other end. Of all these great pace combinations none was more menacing than that of Lindwall and Miller in their prime.

Ray Lindwall had everything : speed, hostility, change of pace, swerve, stamina and superb control. He was an artist in a trade which all too frequently relies on brute force.

How quick was Lindwall? The M.C.C. players who toured Australia in 1946–7 reckoned that he was at his fastest during that trip. Whether that was because they were encountering real speed for the first time since the war, or because bowlers are always a shade faster in Australia than in this country (Frank Tyson provides an example of this) I do not know, but there is no doubt that Ray was still unpleasantly, and often devastatingly, quick when he made his first visit to England in 1948 under Sir Donald Bradman. Personally, I would put him in the same pace category as Wes Hall and Frank Tyson.

I had my first experience of batting against him at Fenners during this tour. Until then I still cherished the hope that I might become a bowler of genuine pace myself. Ray Lindwall's speed compared with my own made the whole idea ridiculous. In addition to his ability in the mechanics of bowling, Ray was capable of frightening good batsmen and absolutely terrifying all but the most courageous or foolhardy of the 'tail', because his speed automatically introduced an element of physical fear. It was obvious that I would have to develop along different lines if I were to

RAY LINDWALL ... the complete fast bowler.

Roy ULLYETT.

have any real chance of establishing myself as an international. For the first and not the last occasion Ray Lindwall was to have a direct bearing upon my own career.

The fast bowler, like the heavyweight boxer, is one of the greatest attractions in the game. Spectators love to see him in full cry, with the prospect of stumps somersaulting out of the ground, the odd delivery rearing past an unfortunate batsman's nose, and the ball thudding into the wicket-keeper's gloves with him standing some twenty paces back. While the fast bowler is operating one feels that something is always liable to happen and even on the most passive of pitches he is quite capable of transforming the course of the game in a very short time. All these things become even more exciting when the bowler concerned has such a glorious approach, body action and follow-through as Ray Lindwall possessed. It is quite impossible to imagine cricket being dull whenever he was bowling.

The run up is one of the most important and exhilarating features of pace bowling. It should start slowly and gradually work up into a crescendo the moment before going into the delivery stride. The ideal body action combines power with grace and gradually fades away into the follow-through. Ray more than fulfilled all these requirements and watching him in action was one of the most satisfying spectacles that the game has produced. It is interesting to note that he avoided the common failing of having an overlong approach which wastes both time and energy. His run up was just under twenty walking paces and never varied, so that the batsman could never pick the bouncer or the slower ball until the very last moment. Many bowlers telegraph their bumper from the moment they start their run – which makes life easy for the batsman – while none of the English fast bowlers since the war, with the exception of Peter Loader, has possessed a slower ball which ought seriously to inconvenience the wary player. One reason for this is that it takes a great deal of practice for anyone with a full arm swing to disguise a really slow delivery and it is a weapon which is far more useful on overseas pitches which are less receptive to movement off the seam. Lindwall's slow ball claimed a number of victims through the batsman being deceived into playing far too soon. In one respect Lindwall might conceivably be criticized for the comparative slowness of his bowling arm. This, combined with his long drag meant that he achieved rather less movement off the seam with an old ball and lift, than a bowler, such as Keith Miller, with a higher action whose arm was perpendicular at the instant of releasing the ball.

Ray was, in fact, the first of the great post-war 'draggers'. At the time this method had a number of practical advantages which outweighed the disadvantage of losing height at the moment of delivery. In particular the Australian umpires did not object if the bowler dropped behind the bowling crease and then dragged through. This meant that the dragger was able to release the ball closer to the batsman than the orthodox bowler, and at great pace this made a considerable difference. The situation reached absurdity when Rorke, another Australian, managed to break the batting crease with his back foot without being no-balled. This and similar cases eventually led to the present law, where the position of the front foot is the deciding factor as to what constitutes a fair delivery.

In England the umpires insisted, as they did with Trueman and Tyson (and all the rest of the imitators) that Ray landed a foot or so behind the bowling crease. Such was his control that he overcame the handicap without any apparent difficulty. The trouble with this method was that umpires often varied in the amount they brought the bowlers back.

I have never encountered a genuinely fast bowler who moved the ball in the air as much, and as late, as Lindwall. In consequence, he was the most devastating exploiter of the new ball and in this respect, the game has never seen his equal.

In all grades of cricket bowlers tend to waste the new ball by not bowling at the stumps. The chief reason is the difficulty of controlling swing. Aim at the off stump and the ball is apt to swerve too early and too much to worry the batsman; switch to the leg stump and the ball refuses to move and the batsman plays it comfortably through the many gaps on the leg side. Ray Lindwall, on the contrary, possessed the rare ability to start to swing the ball *outside* the line of the leg stump and hit the off. I shall always remember how he deceived Reg Simpson with just such a delivery at Lord's in 1953. Reg was very strong off his legs. He attempted to push Lindwall through the on side only to find the ball had served so much and so late that it took the outside edge of his bat and he was caught by Benaud in the gulley.

As a result of his action and wrist at the instant of delivery Ray's natural swing was away from the bat and in common with all great fast bowlers he made the odd ball come back off the seam. However, as a result of a spell in the Lancashire League, he added the in-swinger to his repertoire, something I learned to my cost while collecting one of my more lengthy 'ducks'. I was opening the innings with Sir Len Hutton and after some forty-five minutes in which I had the utmost difficulty in making any contact whatsoever I decided it was time to get off the mark. There was only one fieldsman (Neil Harvey) in front of the bat on the off side and Ray bowled me a near half-volley just wide of the off stump. I attempted a push out into the open spaces only to find the ball had dipped in late, careered through an enormous 'gate', and carried away my middle stump.

Every year, with unfailing regularity, there is a move to return to the old lbw law in the hope that it will bring about more off-side play. If this ever occurred one important point would be the compensating factor to the bowler in the shape of either a slightly smaller ball, or a larger wicket. Some years ago when we were experimenting with a small cricket ball, Ray was asked to demonstrate his skill with one in the nets at Lord's. He gave a splendid exhibition of his exceptional control, by regularly nominating and hitting individual stumps, as well as swinging the ball even more than usual. He made it appear all so simple that I was thankful he was never allowed to operate with a smaller ball in a match. He was more than enough trouble with the standard type.

Although Ray was a cunning, almost Machiavellian exponent of his craft, as a person he was essentially a down to earth, uncomplex character, who would fit naturally into a Hollywood Western, equally at home on the range or in one of those long, boisterous bars. With his stamina, superb physique and lust for life he would have made a superb pioneer in the early days of his country, a man's man, ideal to have around when the going was tough. You could never imagine him needing a psychoanalyst.

Ray was such an outstanding bowler that it is easy to forget he was a fine fielder, a formidable attacking batsman, as well as a distinctly useful Australian Rules footballer. As a batsman he was just the right person to demoralize an attack which was beginning to wilt, or to lead a recovery by bold forthright methods. He hit the ball with a power that was sometimes almost ferocious. With his crouching stance and low grip he was an effective, rather than a stylish performer. His defence was sometimes shaky, especially, like so many of the brotherhood, when confronted by real pace. When I was bowling against him I always wished that I could conjure up sufficient speed to slip him a bouncer of genuinely lethal proportions and follow this with a yorker, tactics which brought Ray so many wickets – in fact his yorker was the most effective I have come across, and he could produce it at will without making the common mistake of occasionally slipping in a half-volley or a full toss. As one would expect from his low grip on the bat and his fine eye he excelled in the cut. Drop the ball just a shade short and it would be speeding to the pickets past third man.

Ray's cricketing career and my own have entwined more than most. He is the only bowler to have put me out of action for any length of time. This occurred in the third Test at Sydney on my first tour. In the previous match Ray had not been at his best and there were suggestions from the Australian press that he should be dropped, a view with which all the English batsmen were in complete agreement. For once the M.C.C. had batted themselves into a reasonable position when I joined my captain, Freddie Brown. Freddie had played with considerable distinction in the second Test, when he had driven the Australian slow bowlers with both effect and relish. He was in the process of repeating the dose, when Lindsay Hassett brought on Ray Lindwall and the Australians at last realized that Freddie, who was primarily a front foot driver, was vulnerable against fast short bowling. Ray tore into the attack, let fly the odd bouncer, hit Freddie on the foot with a very fast, painful yorker and then comprehensively bowled him. Freddie never made another fifty against them. Shortly after one of his deliveries rose sharply from just short of a length. In order not to give a catch, I attempted to play the ball down, but used my thumb instead of the bat. I was not worried until I attempted to grip the handle and found it was not possible. Subsequently an X-ray showed it to be broken and meant that I missed my one and only Test in five tours.

Ray is the only bowler to whom I have ever deliberately given my wicket in international cricket, something which I am not over keen in doing even in club games. This was after we had won the Ashes and were engaged in the final Test of the tour. It was near the close of the final day of a rain-curtailed contest, I was in my eighties and a draw had become inevitable. At the time it was thought that Ray was retiring and he only needed one wicket to bring his grand total up to two hundred. It seemed to me that any bowler, especially a fast bowler, who comes so close certainly deserves to achieve it. As things turned out we had not seen the last of Ray and, ironically enough, it was he who ended my own Test career at Melbourne two series later when he removed me for a 'pair' in our final encounter. Once again I was a sacrificial opener and, in the first innings, was caught off the glove from one that lifted and left me. It would have baffled many batsmen and was certainly far too good for me. I came in on the mark in our second innings and was completely deceived by a late in-swinger after a couple of interesting outers. It was not the way I would have chosen to depart from the international scene, but I did at least have the satisfaction of falling to a great adversary, who was always scrupulously fair and whom I had sometimes been able to frustrate.

If I were asked to sum up Ray's bowling in one word, I would say 'control'. Control over the fundamentals of length and direction. Control over the finer arts of his trade.

14

ALEC BEDSER
'The Big Fella'

Both metaphorically and physically Alec Bedser stands head and shoulders above every other fast medium bowler I have played with or against. He was a truly great bowler who ranks alongside S. F. Barnes and Maurice Tate.

My first encounters with Alec were in charity matches during the war; and I came to know him well during the immediate post-war period of county cricket. In those days he was an honest workman rather than a complete craftsman – a stock bowler who swung the ball into the batsman and was prepared to keep an end going for the whole of the day.

In 1946 England was distinctly short of bowling and Alec was chosen to open our attack. He gained his first cap then and retained his position for the next decade. He was invited to accompany the M.C.C. to Australia in the winter of 1946–7; as Doug Wright was the only other bowler of real class in that team, Alec was given enough work to have killed a smaller or a less stouthearted man. For hour after hour in hot sunshine he plugged steadily away. He never gave up even when the Australians amassed some enormous totals.

Alec was always an exceptionally conscientious cricketer, never content with things as they were, ever striving to improve. He was a true professional, dedicated to his calling, which is why perhaps he is apt to be a rather harsh critic of the younger player who lacks such singleness of purpose. Because of the lost war years he did not reach his peak until 1950. It was from 1950 and for the next four years that the quality of his bowling on all types of pitches and under varying conditions was as near to perfection as any I have encountered.

First and foremost, the 'big fella' believed in the old maxim that it pays to attack the stumps, and he seldom strayed off course. In addition, he always kept an immaculate length. He considered a bad delivery to be an insult to his craft and nobody was meaner when it came to giving batsmen half-volleys or long hops: one in a match he considered over-generous.

Although Alec had a classical action his natural swing was into the bat. Like all the best swerve bowlers he made the ball move very late in its flight and I have lost count of the number of times I have seen players about to drive him through the covers only to find themselves 'bowled through the gate'. He never really employed the out-swinger, but he would push the odd ball away, make it hold its own and use the crease which, taken in conjunction with his deadly 'in-dipper', was more than sufficient.

Batting against Alec provided a fascinating challenge. If I was lucky enough to remain, I was reminded of the privilege for some time to come because the knuckles on my right hand would be sore and bruised as a result of constant jarring. Although Alec was not fast he certainly 'hit the deck' so that he always came off the wicket a shade quicker than one expected, while personally I never picked out his beautifully disguised slower ball until it was too late. He much preferred to have the wicket-keeper standing up, despite the fact that he was quicker than many who always operate with him standing back. He believed it aided his accuracy and restricted the batsman's movement, which more than compensated for the odd missed chance. In this connection he was lucky to have had two exceptional keepers, the brilliant Evans for England and the very dependable and often underrated Macintyre for Surrey. The way they handled his bowling, especially over a nasty lifting track, was quite superb.

The attributes already mentioned would by themselves have ensured Alec a permanent place in cricket history, but in addition he possessed a leg cutter which became a legend and was probably the most devastating ever known. This is a hard delivery to bowl effectively and it took Alec a long time to master. He had four things in his favour: first, he was prepared to practise; secondly, he had the basic control; thirdly, his natural delivery was the in-swinger; fourthly, the size of his hands and the power

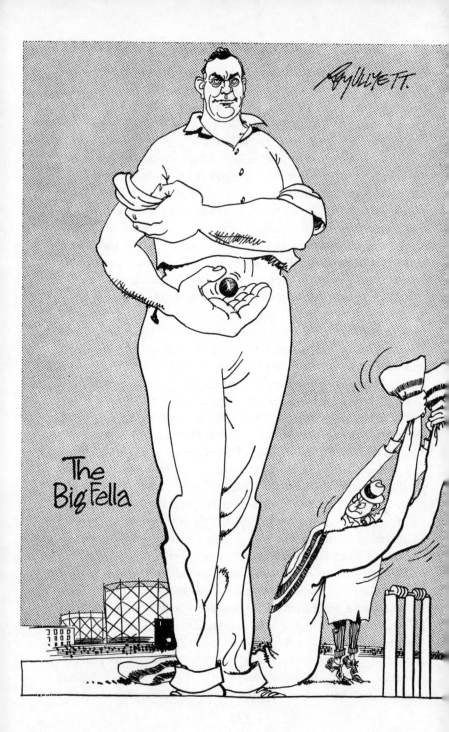

The Big Fella

of his fingers were exceptional. When I measured my fingers against his, the tops of mine were just level with his first knuckle! On a wet or crumbling pitch he was often almost unplayable. What can a batsman do against the ball which pitches leg stump and whips back to hit the top of the off at a lively fast medium?

I was batting once with Doug Insole for Essex against Surrey on a rain-affected wicket at The Oval, when Alec bowled one of the most remarkable overs I have ever seen. Fortunately, I was at the other end. It was a fascinating performance. The ball kept dipping in, pitching around the leg stump and flying over the top of the off. Insole was unable to make any contact with the first five deliveries; and he managed to edge the last ball through the slips at catchable height for four – which brought forth a few well chosen words from Alec about Doug's luck in particular and fate in general.

It is difficult to pick out the highlights of Alec's career, because it contained so many. However, in the 1950–1 M.C.C. tour of Australia, despite lack of class support, Alec turned in a whole series of marvellous performances which, with the exception of the Australian second innings in the first Test, were on fine batting pitches. On that Brisbane 'sticky' the scoreboard read: Australia 0 for 3; and we had them 32 for 7 when they declared. I shared the ball with Alec throughout this session and opened the attack with him throughout the series except when injured. He finished with thirty wickets including five in each innings in the fifth Test at Melbourne which brought us that elusive victory. He was both spearhead and stock bowler, a remarkable combination. In particular he had an almost hypnotic effect on that fine left-hander Arthur Morris, probably because he dipped the new ball away from him so late. This was to continue throughout the next series in England to such an extent that Arthur was to become known as 'Bedser's Bunny'. No one bowler ever troubled him so much and so often.

In 1953 in England Alec was probably the biggest single factor in our regaining the Ashes. He worried everyone with his nagging accuracy, movement in the air and off the pitch and his ability to produce the really devastating delivery even on a docile track.

I cherish the memory of the ball with which he dismissed Lindsay Hassett in 'Bedser's Test Match' at Trent Bridge. Hassett, with over a hundred to his credit, was batting superbly and then Alec ambled up. The ball started outside the off stump, whipped in, pitched leg and just clipped the top of the off. In this game Alec returned the following figures:

First Innings 38·3 overs, 16 maidens, 55 runs, 7 wickets, out of a total of 249

Second Innings 17·2 overs, 7 maidens, 44 runs, 7 wickets, out of a total of 123

It was the best and most devastating piece of sustained fast-medium bowling it has been my privilege to witness and, because I was also a seamer, probably nobody could have appreciated its worth more.

In addition to his bowling Alec was a more than useful tail-end batsman, particularly against pace. I am sure that he would have scored many more runs if he had not been so overworked in other directions. Few lower order players have been able to hit the ball off the back foot with a straight bat more impressively. As a fielder, inevitably, he was not the most agile; however he developed, with his enormous hands, into a safe slip for seam bowlers and it gave me confidence to see him standing there when I was bowling.

Basically, Alec is a straightforward character, honest, kind and absolutely dependable, a man without enemies and universally respected. It is difficult to imagine anyone disliking him. His out-look is decidedly conservative, a shade predictable and perhaps a little limited. This tends to make him suspicious of change and at times even slightly intolerant. His own standards are very high and occasionally rigid, so that sometimes he has difficulty in appreciat-ing another's point of view.

But Alec, of course, has an identical twin, Eric, and they are so close that it is impossible to write objectively about one without the other. It is not merely that they look alike – and it was a long time before I learned to tell them apart – but they think, talk, dress and live as one complete unit. They have a joint bank ac-count and are never happier than when they are in each other's company. Eric is the leader but they never argue because they think alike. I have never encountered such complete harmony between two people; indeed, if you walk down the street with them and start in the middle, by the end of the block you will find yourself on the outside. This almost uncanny affinity was splendidly demonstrated in a Surrey game against Yorkshire, when Tony Lock brought off a typically brilliant catch in the gulley. Alec turned to Norman Yardley and remarked, 'He's a good catcher in the gully, he is'. A minute later Eric strolled in from the outfield, came up to Norman, and used the identical words with the same inflection and tone.

Whenever Alec was invited to tour overseas with the M.C.C. Eric would accompany him on the trip. During the 1946–7 trip Alec lost weight as a result of an especially long and gruelling spell in extreme heat and when Eric stood on the scales they showed that he had lost the same amount, presumably in sympathy. On the following tour the M.C.C. found themselves short of players and Eric was invited to take part in one contest. This provided the supreme test of brotherly love as Eric managed to drop a couple of catches off his other half! When we moved on to New Zealand Eric had to go back to England by ship and so for a month we had the rare experience of getting to know Alec as an individual, rather than as part of a closely knit duo which thinks and acts as one.

One of the many pleasant features of touring is the fact that some firms are generous enough to present the visitors with gifts. When I first went to Australia food was still short in England and we regularly sent home food parcels. Just before we were due to leave it was suggested that it would be wonderful to arrange for an especially fine parcel to go back in the ship with those members of the party who were not travelling to New Zealand. Alec, who always seems to know everyone everywhere, kindly volunteered to organize the operation and I was appointed his junior assistant. Alec produced his diary which contained an enormous list of names, which would have done credit to a contact man, and methodically planned our campaign. The combination of Australian hospitality and Bedser's direction was more than sufficient to guarantee the success of the enterprise.

Alec and Eric joined the Surrey staff together in 1939, just before the war. In those days Alec was a fast-medium in-swinger and Eric a fast-medium away-swinger. Because it soon became apparent that there were too many seamers at The Oval they characteristically decided that one of them would have to concentrate on batting and slow bowling. Because he moved the ball away Eric found he could bowl far better off-breaks than his brother, and so it was he who abandoned seam bowling. If he had continued, I wonder how good he would have become, because initially there was little to choose between them. As it was, Eric developed into a very competent all rounder. If he had played for any other county than Surrey, who at that time had in Laker and Lock two class spinners, he might well have been selected for England.

Both Alec and Eric have always had a healthy regard for money. They appreciate its value and do not like to see it squandered. Inevitably, there are opportunities for sportsmen in the world of commerce, but rather too many expect a return without being willing to supply the effort. This was not the case with the Bedser twins, who worked hard and methodically built up an excellent business. They approached this task with the same dedication and sense of purpose that they had shown to their cricket so that their eventual success was not only deserved, but surprised nobody who knew them.

Alec's tastes are in keeping with his character. He prefers plain food and plenty of it and is happier with beer than with champagne. His sense of humour is ungarnished and somewhat sardonic, while he has a happy knack of producing a pithy homily on the subject of the unkindness of the world to bowlers. During the ill-fated Test in Sydney when the M.C.C. attack had been reduced to three and Alec was trundling down about his fortieth eight-ball over, he suddenly announced to the world at large that he had that day received a letter from the Surrey secretary telling him to look after himself and be ready for the Championship the following summer. His comment was both laconic and typical.

Alec is especially valuable in times of stress and crisis, because he remains calm and unruffled. Only two occasions come to mind

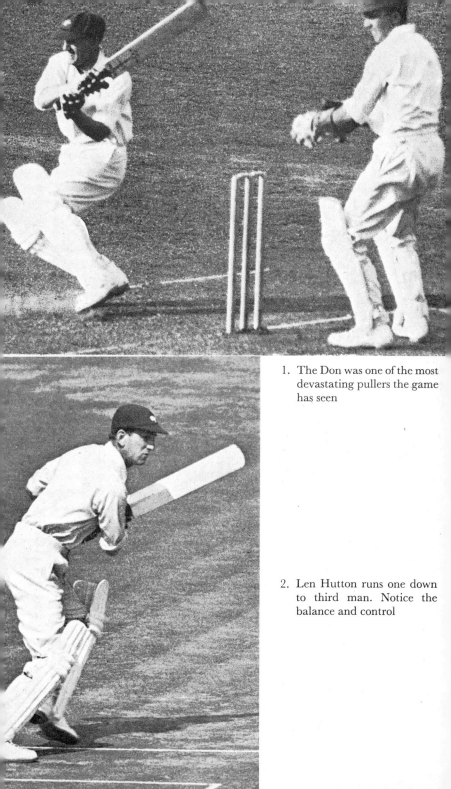

1. The Don was one of the most devastating pullers the game has seen

2. Len Hutton runs one down to third man. Notice the balance and control

3. Hutton and Washbrook, the best opening pair for England since the war

4. Cyril Washbrook square cuts with the bottom hand very much in evidence

5. Bill Edrich, an exciting and effective hooker

6. Denis Compton dabs one down to third man. Note how far back he has gone on to his stumps

. Compton had little use for nets except as pre-season looseners, but here he is playing a drive off his back foot

8. *Top left:* Everton Weekes striking a four past square leg

9. *Top right:* Frank Worrell elegantly square-cutting off the back foot, with four runs written all over the stroke

10. *Left:* Clyde Walcott slashing through the covers on the rise off his front foot, with his typical West Indian gaiety including the right knee on the ground!

11. Tom Graveney hooking Wes Hall to the boundary, Sobers at slip. He is so expert on his front foot that he is even able to hook quick bowling from there

12. Peter May driving power-fully to the on, off his back foot

13. Colin Cowdrey never has to hurry his strokes. Here he has hooked Corling to the boundary perfectly and with time to spare

4. Ken Barrington is exceptionally strong off his legs. Here he plays an on drive-cum-push

15. Ted Dexter – a full-blooded drive off the front foot
with the complete follow-
through

16. In cricket and golf the
Dexter drive has exceptional
power and beauty

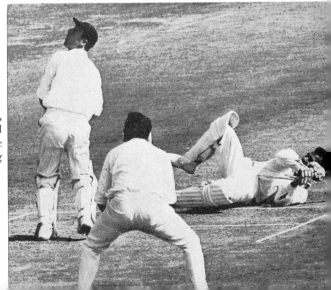

17. The Kanhai special,
a cross between a pull
and a sweep, not to be
found in any coaching
manual

18-19. Ray Lindwall (*above*) going into his delivery stride, and (*below*) just before the moment of delivery, showing his right foot drag

20-21. Alec Bedser's tremendous body action and mighty follow-through

22. Brian Statham was un-
usually supple, and had a
very whippy action

23. Alan Davidson compreh-
sively bowls Brian Statha
with one that moved lat

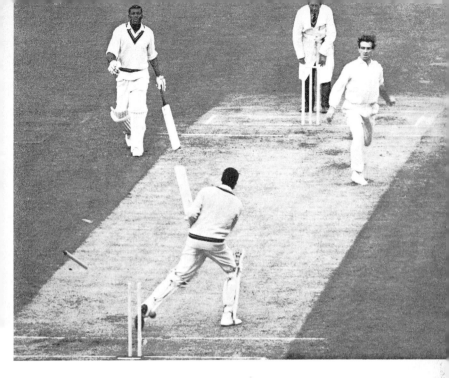

24. Fred Trueman demolishing the 'tail' — Lance Gibbs at the receiving end

25. Trueman has Colin McDonald caught by Godfrey Evans off the outside edge, and gives full vent to his jubilation

26. Jim Laker's body action was classical. He looked over the left arm, came down on a braced left leg, swivelled and even dug a pit with his left foot

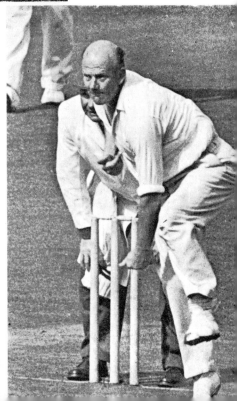

27. Tony Lock, so patently dedicated to the job in hand, removing the enemy

28. Godfrey Evans catching Neil Harvey down the leg side, standing up to Alec Bedser whose pace was a distinctly lively fast-medium

29. Keith Miller, the gay swashbuckling batsman from 'down
under'

30. Richie Benaud weaving his
spells

31. Sobers on the rampage with a completely uninhibited hook

32. Captain traps captain. Brian Close lbw to Sobers, bowling seam

33. A wonderful catcher close to the bat, especially at backward short leg

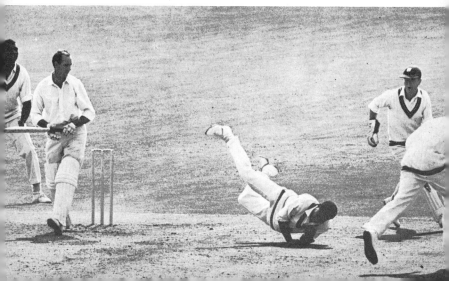

34. Possibly out of character, but fact not fantasy

35. One of my happiest moments. Neil Harvey, caught Bailey bowled Trueman

when I have seen him taken aback. The first was when a batsman in an Australian up-country match, armed with an old, ugly red-handled bat, suddenly smote him out of the ground. The second was on the golf course when his opponent, playing off a 24 handicap, produced 13 birdies in 18 holes.

Alec Bedser bowling was one of cricket's most impressive sights. The big body dripping with sweat, the slow methodical amble up to the crease, the massive head rocking from side to side, and finally the tremendous body action and powerful follow-through. This was cricket at its best.

E

15

J. C. LAKER

'Big Jim'

Coming off the field after England – or more accurately Jim Laker – had heavily defeated the Australians on that dusty travesty of a pitch at Old Trafford in 1956, I kept repeating to myself that it was all a dream. It could not have happened. At the time it was difficult to appreciate that we had witnessed the most remarkable bowling feat in the history of Test cricket. Outside of dreams and of boys' comics, bowlers do not take nineteen wickets in a match, let alone in an international match. Even now, it does not seem to make sense.

What made it more incredible was that, at the other end, Tony Lock only managed to secure one victim although the ball was frequently turning almost square. Tony, as always, had tried desperately – perhaps almost too desperately – to share in the spoils. The rivalry between this great Surrey pair did not permit intentional generosity when it came to the matter of wickets!

'Big Jim' Laker is the finest off-spinner I have played with or against. On hard wickets overseas perhaps Hugh Tayfield and Lance Gibbs have looked his equal, but under all conditions he was in a class of his own. He was an artist. First, he had exceptional control. Accuracy of line and length is the fundamental of all categories of bowling, but to none is it more important than the off-spinner. On occasions a fast full toss will take a wicket, while many a batsman has holed out off a leg-breaking long-hop, but the off-spinner cannot afford inaccuracies of this nature, because he has to rely so much on his short leg fieldsmen, who must be prepared to stand perilously close to the batsman. A bad ball immediately puts them in considerable danger. Even if they avoid being hit, a series of indifferent deliveries will very quickly destroy their confidence. Then they will edge away instead of forward and so greatly reduce their effectiveness. Short leg has never been my favourite position, but I was always happy to stand there for Jim Laker as his control reduced my chances of being struck to a minimum. I found I could afford to station myself considerably closer to the wicket than with any other bowler of his type. This made all the difference when trying to make a catch off a purely defensive stroke. I was at short leg to Jim when he once turned a Test trial, at Bradford, into a farce by taking eight of The Rest's players for only two runs. It was a fascinating experience to watch from such a close quarter this classic off-spinner at work on a helpful pitch. He may not have made the ball talk, but he certainly made it fizz, lift and turn.

Second, Laker's body action was almost classical. He looked over the left arm, came down on a braced left leg, swivelled, and even dug a pit with his left foot. Third, he spun his off-break sufficiently to make it bend on perfect pitches. Fourth, he was equally at home over or round the wicket. When he was abroad he operated chiefly from over, but on a pitch responsive to turn, he went round. Fifth, he had the ability to make the ball *leave* the bat off the pitch without any perceptible change of action. I was not alone in being unable to pick the one 'that went with his arm'. His subtle variations of flight and spin were a continued source of delight to the connoisseur. He learnt to recognize and exploit the foibles of individual batsmen and was able to adapt his techniques to different circumstances. Although his rewards in terms of wickets were inevitably greater on a 'sticky' or a 'crumbler' at The Oval, Jim was still liable to worry the finest players in the world on that hard, fast batting paradise at Sabina Park.

I have never been a good player of off-spin bowling and in my early days found facing Jim something of a nightmare. I was a regular Laker 'bunny'. I would go in, push down the line, and then a delivery would lift and turn. This would take my inside edge and the catch would be gratefully gobbled up by either Surridge or Lock, lurking close at short leg. This became so unpleasantly predictable that I eventually decided to take some positive action. Confronted by Jim at The Oval on a pitch where the ball was biting, I realized that if I did not change my tactics I might

just as well remain in the pavilion. Knowing that Jim's length was near perfect, I gave him the occasional charge which meant that he could not afford to drop every ball on the same spot. The outcome was that I did manage to take a few runs and although batting remained difficult it was not entirely impossible. He still continued to capture my wicket, but from that moment on I occasionally had my revenge and on one occasion at Southend I did make a hundred against Surrey. I was in the seventies when I was joined by our number eleven, Gerry Jerman, a good club bowler, playing his first game for the County. I managed to retain the strike for several overs, but eventually Gerry was called upon to receive his first ball in County cricket from Jim. His shot was impressive: a massive mow, which sent the ball straight into the lake and made me wonder whether he really needed any protection.

It has been said that Laker did not like to be hit. I have yet to encounter a bowler who did! Sometimes certainly, in his early days, he did wilt under such treatment, but by the time he had reached his peak, it was well nigh impossible to 'collar' him for any length of time. When he went to Australia under Peter May some of the Aussie batsmen were thirsting for revenge, because Jim had so mesmerized them on the turning English pitches. They longed to set about him on their own good batting wickets, yet although they attempted this (most of them holing out in the deep) they were noticeably unsuccessful. He had become too great a craftsman and the wise soon appreciated this.

Most slow bowlers take a considerable time to reach their peak, and Jim was no exception. There was no comparison between the callow off-spinner who played against the Australians in 1948 and the polished artist he later became. Perhaps he was unlucky to be chosen at this stage, before he was fully ready for international cricket, since it may have been the cause for the selectors subsequently taking such a long time to appreciate his talents. One of the most surprising features of his career was that he was not selected more often for England. He was a permanent member of the national side for only a comparatively short period.

He obviously ought to have gone to Australia in 1950, when we went without an off-spinner and Tattersall was flown out as a late replacement, while his omission from the 1954–5 tour under Sir Len Hutton was an even bigger mystery. By this time the myth that off-break bowlers were unlikely to succeed out there had been finally exploded and we took Appleyard and McConnon. Possibly the fact that he was born a Yorkshireman had some connection, as temperamentally Hutton and Laker were so far removed, and yet in some ways so close, that a conflict of ideas was bound to occur from time to time. This was very obvious in the West Indies in 1953–4. Hutton was inclined to overestimate the importance of speed and underestimate the power of spin. Nevertheless, Jim Laker bowled exceptionally well on some beautiful batting wickets.

The majority of outstanding players are apt to be individualists. Jim was something of an introvert, at times withdrawn and even moody. A perfectionist himself, he was inclined to be intolerant of the mediocre, but he was always prepared to take pains to assist anyone willing to listen and to work. His Yorkshire upbringing undoubtedly influenced him, both as a cricketer and as a man. The north takes its sport seriously. Although northerners have a masked sense of humour, it does not stretch to such things as loose deliveries, suicidal swings and dropped catches, unless, of course, the perpetrator is a member of the opposition. It followed that Jim approached the game with a determination to succeed. His job was to take wickets and win matches. He had no wish, or intention, of becoming a good loser, he wanted to be a regular winner and with both England and Surrey this normally occurred. Surrey with their international attack expected victory and he found it somewhat strange when he later joined Essex where this was a comparatively rare event and the outlook was inevitably lighter-hearted.

The shrewd, calculated approach, which was such a feature of his cricket, he brought also to his business affairs. It has come as no surprise to those who knew him that he has proved to be highly successful.

The fact that he was so frequently ignored by the selectors probably increased Jim's somewhat sardonic outlook. He knew he was the finest bowler of his type in the country, but he was still overlooked when it came to inclusion in the national eleven, and this can only have added to his inborn cynicism. He cultivated an ultra-casual approach and often gave the impression of being bored with the proceedings. In consequence he was an obvious target for criticism when he was not meeting with success. People were misled into thinking that he was simply not interested, and failed to take into account that Jim's outward attitude in times of stress was exactly the same as in moments of triumph. Even when he was collecting those nineteen Australian scalps, he gave no indication of the thrill he must have felt. He was one of the least demonstrative bowlers.

The more I played with Jim the more I began to understand his complex character and appreciate the significance of his mannerisms. There was that slightly disdainful hitch of the trousers before he commenced his measured approach to the wicket. When he was hit to the boundary, he would instinctively give his magic and very enlarged spinning finger a contemplative inspection and a little gentle massage. No bowler enjoys having a catch put down. Some curse, some rave, some cry, some gesticulate, but these actions were too melodramatic for Jim. He merely stood there and waited for the return of the ball, quietly tapping a foot, and massaging the finger, and lifting his eyes upwards as if asking justice for bowlers and perhaps suggesting that it would not be amiss if a thunderbolt should strike the offending fieldsman – a delightfully underplayed little cameo.

Normally Jim Laker did not worry over much about his batting although, in common with most bowlers, he was more than prepared and even willing to discuss its merits with anyone foolish enough to listen. However, he did have the ability to score runs on occasions, especially if they were really essential. For Surrey this was seldom necessary, as they had normally won before he had even had to put on his pads. However, for England against the Australians in 1948 he did make 63 out of a total of 165. He had an extremely high back lift with such a pronounced loop that his bat often failed to come down completely straight, consequently he was frequently caught behind the wicket; indeed his outside edge was said to be the best in the business! His most impressive shot was the cover drive which he could execute with almost classical perfection, while in general he was more at ease against spin than against speed.

I have shared in several partnerships with Jim and perhaps the most valuable was at Leeds against the Australians. The exact number of runs we put on or, to be more accurate, that Jim scored, is immaterial, as my own share was minute, but it did the necessary job of holding up the enemy. The one thing I knew, when I batted with Jim, was that there was never any danger of being run out, simply because he did not run. He was content to amble along at a regular steady pace between the wickets, like a stage coach at a ceremonial parade.

The most dramatic moment of Jim's batting that I saw occurred in Trinidad when he was hit under the eye by a bouncer from King. That a bowler should bounce them at Jim was unusual and that he should be hit almost unique. It was, in fact, an unpleasant injury which opened up his eyebrow and I shall never forget his spectacular departure from the field in a swaying zig-zag, clasping his eye with the blood dripping down, and pursued by the entire West Indies side who were trying to come to his assistance.

In the field Jim was a safe gulley, but not the fastest nor the most agile mover. He was nicknamed the 'Tiger' for his work in this department and on more than one occasion surprised everyone, including himself, by justifying it.

After the Peter May tour to Australia Jim Laker, who had enjoyed a truly magnificent Benefit, decided to retire from the game and also to produce a book which turned out to be highly controversial. The outcome was that he was banned from first class cricket and that his honorary membership of both Surrey and the M.C.C. was revoked. It was sad, especially when one realized that it had happened to the finest off-spinner this country has produced and I believe Jim bitterly regretted his action. After a considerable time in cricket purgatory, however, he was adjudged cleansed. It so happened that about then I attended some cricket function with him up in the north. After a distinctly festive evening we journeyed home together on the following day. I mentioned that Essex was short of spin and what an asset he would be if it were possible for him to help us out on occasions.

Much to my delight he said that he was willing to do this and the following summer he was specially registered and came to play for us as an amateur. Unfortunately, not all the members of my committee were as enthusiastic as myself at acquiring such a great bowler and such a draw for nothing. I wonder what the reaction would be of any professional soccer club, who suddenly found themselves in the position of being able to sign on a genuine star performer on a free transfer and also did not have to pay him a salary!

Although Jim was never able to play regularly for Essex and was in the twilight of his career, he still showed that he was the best of his kind in the country. We won some matches, which we could never have hoped to do without his presence, and Brian Taylor's wicket-keeping improved to a marked degree!

In his brief stay with Essex, Laker gave many examples of his mastery. His very first game was against Derby at Valentines Park. He had been out of cricket for a long time and many people, forgetting that there is no substitute for genuine class, were doubtful about how he would perform. It did not take long to find out. The very first ball he bowled dropped on the spot, turned sharply, popped, hit the inside edge, and the catch was comfortably dropped by Gordon Barker at short leg, who quite simply had had no experience of standing there to that category of bowling. Afterwards Gordon complained that this mistake earned him bigger headlines than if he had made a century!

Another example occurred in Leicester on an exceptionally dead pitch which took a little spin. The batsman was a young, inexperienced left-hander to whom Jim bowled round the wicket. The first three deliveries were given a forward defensive stroke. The fourth was slower and higher and was dealt with in a like manner. The fifth was much shorter and much faster. It simply fizzed even off that dead track and went 'on with the arm'. Instinctively the batsman went back only to find himself plumb lbw before he realized what had happened. He came in again in the second innings and the result was a replica of the first, except that, on this occasion, I was already appealing before the ball left Jim's hand.

16

BRIAN STATHAM
The Greyhound

If, from the past fifteen years, you asked all the county captains to name the fast bowler they would most like to have in their side, the majority would choose Brian Statham. In addition to his exceptional ability as a bowler, he is absolutely reliable, never temperamental, and is prepared to bowl his heart out irrespective of pitch or conditions. In other words, he is a great team man as well as a great fast bowler.

I first met Brian Statham in Sydney in 1951, when he and Roy Tattersall were flown out as replacements for Doug Wright and myself who were both on the injured list. Because of my broken thumb I was the only member of the M.C.C. party who was in Sydney when their plane arrived, so it fell to me to look after them before they flew on to join the main group. Both were understandably pale, nervous and excited while Brian seemed very shy. That night we had our first drink together. Since then I have supped ale with him in various parts of the world, and there are few better companions, cheerful, thirsty and never dull.

Statham's belated selection was very largely due to a glowing report by Len Hutton on how well he had bowled in the Roses match of the previous summer. Incidentally, this showed excellent judgement on Hutton's part. At the time I was sceptical about sending out a young 'quickie' whose first class experience was limited to a handful of county games. Brian was not then a truly fast bowler, being closer to fast-medium. In Australia he did not meet with a great deal of success but he was certainly not a failure while his accuracy, which was to be such a feature of his bowling, was already apparent.

Brian Statham is easy-going and rather lazy by nature, two characteristics unusual in a fast bowler. Most pacemen possess an

inborn aggressiveness which helps to supply them with the necessary 'bite'. Some carry their dislike for opposing batsmen to the
extent of literally hating them. When a batsman has the temerity
to hit them to the boundary, they think how delightful it would
be if they could fell him with a bouncer. It is an understandable
outlook and colleagues often deliberately try to stir up this hate
relationship, but it never worked with Brian. He liked people,
even opposing batsmen.

It is extremely irritating for a quick bowler to see a chance go
down, especially if he has been pounding away for an hour or so
in the heat without reward. In these circumstances some bowlers
give vent to their feelings, while others simply wilt, but Brian would
merely shrug his shoulders and continue with the job in hand. Of
all the fast bowlers I have played with and against he remained
the most imperturbable. Even when he had beaten, but not dismissed, a batsman four times in one over, as happened on one
occasion on a batting paradise in the West Indies, he just gave a
somewhat rueful chuckle and carried on. Not for him the extravagant gestures, the flow of colourful language and the cries to
heaven for justice.

I have only seen Brian ruffled on very rare occasions. Once
was at Melbourne when he had brilliantly bowled England back
into the game, taking 5 for 57 in twenty-eight eight-ball overs.
Justifiably, he felt he had done enough to take off his cricket
boots, put on his slippers and relax with a cigarette and a glass
of beer. But, alas, England batted in such a depressingly spineless
fashion that we were shot out for only 87. Brian had to bat and
bowl again the same day. He was not amused.

Brian Statham is often compared with his great international
partner, Freddie Trueman, and inevitably there is considerable
difference of opinion as to who was the finer – which does not
depend upon whether you support the White or the Red Rose.
Tom Graveney said he preferred to bat against Brian rather than
Fred. His reason was that Fred was more unpredictable. You
knew, when facing Brian, exactly what to expect. In other words,
Brian was a shade more accurate, but Fred more liable to produce the unplayable delivery. As far as I am concerned I do not

His ability to toss the World's best
pancakes at any hour of the night
was somewhat overshadowed by
his International reputation as the
most accurate of fast bowlers.

Roy ULLYETT.

relish facing either, but I would sooner bat against Freddie because his percentage of deliveries which I had a chance of scoring from was fractionally higher. When I was facing Brian I could never see where or how I was going to make a run. Ball after ball would pitch just short of a length on, or a fraction outside the off stump. Occasionally a delivery would appear over pitched, but it was always a designed yorker and not the wanted half-volley.

Colin Cowdrey's reactions are identical to Graveney's and opinion among the Essex players split down the middle. Everyone prefers to have both these bowlers on their side!

Pacemen are always more formidable when they can operate in pairs. Because of his phlegmatic and unselfish approach Brian made an ideal partner. At international level he has shared the new ball with both Trueman and Tyson and both these couplings proved highly successful. Brian did not worry if he had to operate up the hill and into the wind, he simply kept on bowling fast and straight. His exceptional accuracy ensured that runs were always at a premium and was one of the main reasons why he was such a great help to his partner. The maxim of his attack has always been : if they miss I hit. Certainly over the years Brian has been indirectly responsible for a large number of wickets at the other end. On more than one occasion I have dismissed a batsman who was so delighted to have escaped temporarily from Brian that he took an unnecessary risk.

Statham has always been more of a seamer than a swing bowler, indeed even with the new ball he seldom moved it appreciably in the air. This was largely due to his body action which was, perhaps, a shade too open for the purist, but his high right arm and the way it chased his left arm across his body until checked by his left hip were copy-book. Besides being double-jointed, Brian was unusually supple, and this has helped to give him the whippy delivery which comes off the pitch a shade faster than the batsman expects. Because of his basic action, most of his deliveries tended to move into the right-handed batsman, but occasionally he made one leave off the seam. He bowled an utterly bemused Jeff Stollmeyer with just such a ball on a perfect pitch in a Caribbean Test. It pitched around middle and leg and clipped the top of the off. It would have bowled anyone in the world; a broth of a ball.

Unlike many fast bowlers, Statham has never been 'bouncer happy'. He used the bumper as a very occasional shock ball, and if I were to make a criticism I would say that it might have profited him sometimes to have tried a few more. He also did not believe in letting the 'tail' have one, as he reckoned he ought to be able to bowl them without recourse to fear and violence. He was usually right, but again it might have occasionally paid to have slipped in a bouncer when they were proving unusually obdurate and holding up the proceedings.

Watching Brian stride forth to bat was always one of cricket's happier moments. On the way he would normally pause to pass a few pleasantries with the opposition, before taking a largely perfunctory guard. He would next somewhat optimistically scan the more remote areas of the ground and then was prepared to do battle. His innings might not last long, but it was usually entertaining. Brian was an unconventional left-handed bat with a good eye, who relied mainly on aggressive strokes and did not believe in getting behind the line. His defence was almost entirely limited to a somewhat diffident forward push, but his attacking shots were varied and colourful, including a delightfully rustic mow to leg, a surprisingly classical cover drive, a powerful slash, and an absolutely invaluable edge, both inside and out. On one never-to-be-forgotten occasion in the fourth Test in South Africa, Brian, in partnership with Peter Loader, gave a superb exhibition of 'edgemanship' against Heine and Adcock with the new ball. For forty-eight minutes they snicked 'em here and they snicked 'em there, until I was close to tears and the opposing bowlers to apoplexy.

Brian's supple build and speed over the ground, combined with a wonderful throwing arm, made him an exceptional outfielder. In addition he had a superb pair of hands. Once the ball was in the air and he was anywhere in the vicinity the bowler could afford to relax.

Statham possessed two nicknames, 'Greyhound' and 'George'. The former was doubtless derived from his pace over the ground, loping stride and lean appearance. In his early days he looked deceptively slight, although he always weighed considerably more than people imagined. The origin of 'George' is somewhat obscure, but it suited him. 'George', after all, is a friendly, homely name, and Brian is essentially a friendly, homely person – indeed as far as Brian was concerned, the one serious snag about touring overseas was the long time he had to be away from his family and the home he loved.

I cannot recall anyone who did not like Statham as an individual, as well as admiring him as a bowler. This is rare in a sport which is frequently cut-throat and where somewhat malicious gossip flourishes. It followed that Brian made a wonderful tourist. He was even-tempered, enjoyed his food and his ale, threw a nifty dart, relished an informal party, especially one where he could remove his shoes, and never caused anyone any trouble. In addition, he possessed a keen sense of humour and a dry wit. He had the habit of producing a succinct comment on life in general when, for example, we were just about to board a plane at some uncivilized hour in the morning. He managed to smoke a surprising quantity of cigarettes, was prepared to saunter leisurely, and not too seriously, around a golf course, though he preferred a putting green, liked a game of tennis, at which he was distinctly useful, and appreciated a day at the races whether he won or lost. Perhaps he was a shade lacking in ambition, but he possessed that priceless virtue, charity.

The only problem which Brian posed for a manager – although once to my great amusement, an amusement not perhaps entirely shared by the captain of the ship, he did manage to delay our sailing from Aden as a result of the hospitality of the troops stationed there – was to get him up in the morning. He really appreciated his bed and much preferred to have a cough, a cigarette and a cup of tea in his room than to rise for a formal breakfast.

He was never by nature, or inclination, an enthusiastic trainer. Neither Brian nor I was ever able to raise much enthusiasm for P.T. on board ship and we both found deck quoits infinitely more satisfactory than the energetic deck tennis.

I have always enjoyed nets, at least when they are well organized, and without doubt Brian was my favourite net bowler. I have always taken strong exception to being hit while practising and therefore will not face anyone likely to do this. On the Len Hutton tour I refused to have Frank Tyson in my net, because his length was not altogether trustworthy, but Brian Statham of course was accuracy personified. He was prepared to send down any type of ball the batsman required and helped me enormously. He himself seldom bothered about batting in the nets unless specially commanded.

Brian was endowed with a wiry toughness and a stamina which enabled him to bowl long spells without too much strain. He kept fit by bowling, rather than by training in order to be fit to bowl. Because he could keep going for over after over without losing much of either his pace or his accuracy, and because he never moaned, there was an understandable tendency to bowl him too much. Fortunately his vitality allowed him to recover remarkably quickly from this mistreatment. However on one occasion it did leave its mark. This was at Lord's in 1955. As usual he had already sent down a goodly quantity of overs for Lancashire and England that season, when he was called upon to bowl unchanged throughout the whole of the South African second innings. He finished with 7 wickets for 39 overs. I doubt whether he has ever bowled better and it rates as one of the great sustained fast bowling feats. It won us the match, but it was a year before Brian was quite himself again.

It is always an asset if a member of a touring party has a party piece which he can trot out on the appropriate occasion. Brian Statham's particular accomplishment was decidedly unusual and considerably more wholesome than most! He had the ability, at any hour of the night, to make the most delicious pancakes. He tossed these with the nonchalance of a super-chef and his drops were even fewer than on the cricket field. I have sampled his pancakes in all parts of the world and at the oddest times, but for the *moment suprême* I would choose an evening in Australia when he was given the freedom of an army kitchen with scores of eggs and gallons of milk at his disposal. He went on for over after over and must have produced enough to satisfy a battalion. I have never eaten quite so many pancakes at one sitting!

17

F. S. TRUEMAN

'Ferocious Fred'

A few winters ago a number of us were lying contentedly on the beach at the Tower Isle Hotel in Jamaica. The sun was shining and the sea was that translucent blue which is such an outstanding feature of the Caribbean. Happy and relaxed we thought of our less fortunate friends back home in an English January. One of the more energetic members of our party cajoled us into joining him in a trip by speed boat down to the Jamaican Hilton, and this developed into one of the most enjoyable and hilarious days of my life.

The somewhat spray-splattered group which eventually disembarked there and made its way to a colourful bar on the beach included Fred and Enid Trueman. Everyone was babbling contentedly when we were joined by an American who had learned from the bar-tender that there were a number of cricketers amongst us, including Trueman, news of whose prowess had penetrated even the United States. The American, obviously fascinated by our strange game, asked Fred, of all people, 'Does an English pitcher ever move the ball?'

Fred, of course, when bowling, possesses the most vivid imagination I have encountered. He is convinced that each ball he delivers is full of venom and artistry. One should never make the mistake of congratulating him, for instance, after he has removed the middle stump of some terrified tail-ender – who anyway was treading on the square leg umpire's toes—with a straight half-volley, because this will provide him with the opportunity of giving a graphic account of that particular delivery; how it dipped in late and then whipped back off the seam. Therefore Fred's reply to that unsuspecting American, was, with the aid of a convenient orange, to hold forth on the intricacies of seam and swing bowling for at least half an hour, scarcely pausing to draw breath. It was a masterful exposition. And undoubtedly Fred's very conviction that every ball he delivers is doing something – and because he is always expecting to remove the opposition and is decidedly perplexed and often highly irritated if they fail to fall – has helped to make him one of the greatest fast bowlers the world has seen.

If anyone queries this assessment of Fred Trueman he has probably not been fortunate enough (or unfortunate, according to one's point of view) to face him in his prime! Examine, however, his Test record, for over a long period figures are a positive proof of ability. In Test cricket, the highest category of the game, Trueman has taken over 300 wickets, more than anyone in cricket history and, what is of even greater significance, he has captured these in only about sixty Test matches. This means he has taken over five wickets per game, an astonishing performance. To average five in county cricket represents a magnificent haul – even on some of the indifferent pitches of the past decade – but on Test pitches, which are normally very good, and against the most accomplished batsmen in the world it is a shattering performance.

In addition to Fred's belief in himself he also expects his fellow fieldsmen to possess supernatural powers when he is bowling. On one occasion in the West Indies his bouncer was hooked viciously, nearly decapitating the unlucky short leg in its jet-propelled flight to the boundary. At the end of the over even I was surprised when he castigated the fielder for putting down yet another chance. He went on to enumerate in detail how he had suffered in this fashion from the opening match of the tour, so that one can easily appreciate what his comments are likely to be if a teammate should grass a really simple chance.

Trueman was a young tearaway fast bowler when I first met him; but he possessed a superb body action and this, combined with his strong physique, suggested that he must surely develop into an outstanding bowler. These attributes have also ensured that he has been able to last much longer than most and has suffered fewer injuries in the process. However, in addition to its effectiveness, the Trueman run-up, body action, and impressive

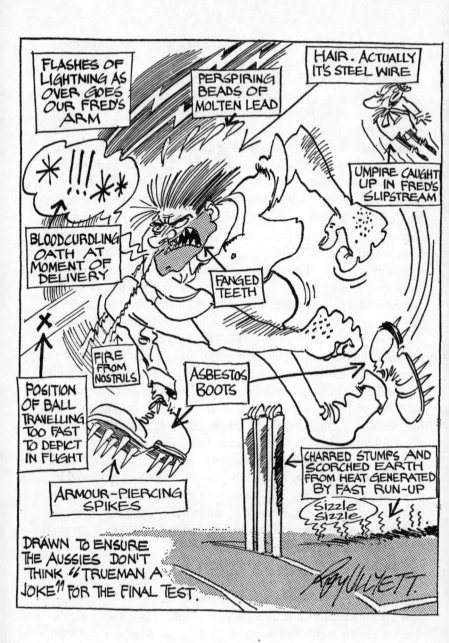

follow-through are things of beauty as well as power. There have been few more stimulating sights since the war than Fred, complete with ferocious scowl, flowing black mane, plus every theatrical gesture in the book (and some that are not) on the warpath. It had everything – flying stumps, disciplined strength, primitive force and the drama that comes whenever a great artist is the central figure on the stage.

Although he had played earlier and indicated his potential, it was not until 1951 that he really established himself as an opening bowler in the finest traditions of Yorkshire cricket, fast and always hostile, with a big heart and backside to match. In the following year he burst upon the international scene in devastating fashion and from that moment he has remained one of the game's most controversial, successful and colourful figures. Many of the Indians in 1952 were plainly terrified by his pace and hostility and retreated abjectly as he tore through their batting. Fred is excessively volatile by nature and his gestures must be among the most expressive ever, while he has never made any secret of the fact that he loathes batsmen, except when they are back in the hutch.

Throughout his career with Yorkshire Fred has not had sufficient help with the new ball at the other end. The county has tried numerous bowlers during the past fifteen years without finding him the ideal partner and this has meant that too much work has been thrust on him, but it says much for his physique that he has been able to maintain his pace and form for so long despite sending down more than 1,000 overs per year in county cricket alone, without taking into account the many Tests and tours.

As with wine, Fred improved with age. He lost a fraction of his pace, but gained in control, cunning and bouquet. In his early days he gave the impression of expecting to blast out every batsman irrespective of their ability or the state of the pitch. Bouncers were despatched with a liberality that reduced their effectiveness. In striving for additional pace, his length and direction sometimes strayed, and this was liable to prove expensive against top class players. This was especially true when he made his first trip to the West Indies in 1953–4. In those days he was raw and naïve both on and off the field. He certainly made a number of mistakes, but sometimes he was unfairly blamed. He was a genuine and sometimes frighteningly fast bowler in the early 1950s, but he did not reach his peak and become a legend until his vintage years from 1958 to 1964. In this period he proved himself to be devastating at home and also on the less sympathetic tracks in Australia and the West Indies, and against fine batsmen.

Fred's action helped him to move the ball away from the bat and it followed that his natural delivery was the out-swinger. With experience he learned to make the best possible use of a pitch which was favourable to seam and, off a shortened run, experimented successfully at cutting the ball at a slightly reduced speed. On all wickets and in all conditions, it is doubtful whether there has ever been a more complete fast bowler. He had fire, aggressiveness, pace, control, a glorious action, as well as that limitless confidence in his own ability.

One of the more important and significant changes that has taken place in county cricket since the war is the realization that it is not sufficient merely to make runs or to take wickets : in addition everyone must, or ought to be, at least, an adequate fieldsman. Formerly players, especially pace bowlers, were tolerated even if they were liabilities in the field. Fred fitted ideally into the new conception, because he was a brilliant all-round fieldsman who was equally at home close to the wicket or in the deep. He had quick reactions, agility, a remarkably safe pair of hands and a throw of sufficient power to justify everyone on the other side of the wicket backing up. When Trueman and Statham opened the bowling for England, the captain was in the happy position of knowing that besides having a wonderful speed bowling combination, who worked even better in double harness, he also possessed two brilliant fieldsmen.

Fred is a natural cricketer and it follows that, in addition to his bowling and fielding he was also able to make runs, though perhaps not as many as he imagined he should. By inclination and character he is an uninhibited hitter who is convinced that he is capable of flaying opposing bowlers irrespective of their quality all over the ground. In truth his range of strokes is limited and he relies largely on a forward defensive jab, a powerful drive, a square cut, a productive edge, a push off the legs, and his *pièce de résistance,* a belligerent cross-batted mow that is liable to send the ball anywhere. Fred has a fine eye and when he connects is liable to hit the ball a very long way. If only he had learned to swing straight his aggregate of runs must have been considerably higher.

I was batting with Fred while he made one of the few centuries of his career. This was at Scarborough for England, which I was captaining against Young England, and he gave a ferocious display of hitting and reached 100 not out in only 67 minutes. My own share in the stand was minute, although I like to think that I did on occasions manage to engineer the strike for him. It was a tremendous exhibition of fierce slogging which sent the ball to every part of the ground and often outside it. Both edges were employed effectively and by the time he had completed his 100 and I was able to declare, I was very close to exhaustion because of our ceaseless running between the wickets, and close too to hysterics because of Fred's asides, the vocal support of a delirious crowd, and the originality of some of the shots.

Fred is not afraid to face pace bowling himself, although he is prepared to indicate forcibly that he is a paid-up member of the 'Fast Bowlers' Union' and therefore ought not to be subjected to any short lifting deliveries. On his final tour with the M.C.C. to the West Indies, when he bowled quite beautifully, he was able to play Wesley Hall quietly with his weight on his front foot, while the recognized batsmen were forever weaving and ducking. However, when Essex played Yorkshire I always liked to drop one short at Fred, even when advancing years made it non-lethal, for it was always fun to hear what he had to say on the matter.

People who know nothing about cricket have heard the name Trueman. He can be read in print, he is heard on the radio, and is seen on television. He is in constant demand to open *fêtes,* to speak at dinners, which he does very well, to serve on panels, to advertise and to attend functions. He has in fact become a celebrity in his own right, for he possesses a strong character, blunt, forthright and not overburdened with tact. His cricket career has almost inevitably been punctuated with and coloured by skirmishes with the authorities. The general public always has a soft spot for individual rebels, and these rows have increased his popularity. In addition to creating a rebel image – sometimes, it must be admitted, without a cause – Fred also became a comedian. He is the best story-teller I have toured with. 'Ferocious', indeed, has an enormous repertoire of involved tales which he puts across in his deep northern tones with great relish and considerable skill. He can be, and often is, very funny, even if, by the end of a long tour, he tends to become a shade exhausting. I was particularly impressed when he gave an impromptu cabaret turn at a hotel in Jamaica to an audience of which ninety per cent were American. It would not have disgraced a professional comic!

On the field Fred has livened many a session, with some clowning, especially when batting, which has ranged from the mundane to the inspired, but the odd succinct comments he makes are usually even more amusing. Many Truemanisms, like his remark to the Rev. David Sheppard after missing yet another 'dolly' – 'For goodness sake put your hands together, Rev. and pray like the rest of us' – have become classics. In fact there is a danger that every funny aside that has ever been made will end up being ascribed to Fred. One of his milder, less ribald comments occurred when both West Indies' batsmen were using runners and we had the odd sight of four batsmen together out in the middle. The umpires passed through our dressing room on their way out to restart play after the tea interval, and just behind them was a white-coated attendant. 'Ah, Sid,' said Fred, 'I see you've brought your ——— runner with you.' It is hard to recapture the timing or the situation, but it was a gem in its own way.

Fred attracts incidents like honey attracts a bee. Once at Hull Essex were playing Yorkshire. It was an unpleasant day at the very start of the season and on a slow wicket Fred had not moved into top gear. Towards the close of play he was put on to bowl a second spell, a tactical move by his skipper which did not have Fred's complete approval. However, during his first over I, as non-striker, watched while a colleague touched a wide, gentle, long-hop into the wicket-keeper's hands and the next batsman was comprehensively yorked first ball. The following player, not famed for his performances against pace, was on a hat-trick. He took guard, Fred decided that his long run was indicated, and I then decided to take an active part in the proceedings. My appeal against the light was immediately upheld and we all left the field, including the Yorkshire side, close to tears, apart from 'Ferocious' who was still limbering up in the far distance. His comments were extremely to the point, but he did not get that hat-trick.

Fred Trueman, comedian, personality and very great cricketer, would always be essential in my side and one of my first choices. It has been an unforgettable, and frequently a hilarious experience to have played with and against him on so many occasions. Our careers have intertwined so much that a high percentage of my happiest memories are linked with him. He had me convulsed the first time he related his story of the knight in shining armour, although I think he was perhaps even funnier on the subject of his omission from the M.C.C. side to tour South Africa, ostensibly on account of advancing years, especially when Ian Thomson of Sussex who was older was eventually included. We had played Yorkshire on a very fast pitch at Leyton soon after the touring team had been picked and 'Ferocious's' dislike for the selectors was temporarily transferred to opposing batsmen. He decided to 'slip himself' and prove conclusively that he was still the fastest and most hostile bowler in the country. He was very convincing, bowling with great fire and hostility, and the ball frequently flew through at head height and really thudded into the wicket-keeper's gloves. One Essex batsman, the comparatively inexperienced Fred Wrightson, attempted a hook and was only partially into his stroke when he was hit in the face and carried off. I went in next and found blood and teeth still on the wicket which made life all the more exciting and batting something of a challenge. Just before the luncheon interval I ducked a Trueman bouncer which failed to rise as much as expected, with the result that I was hit on the back of the head. Remembering the old boxing adage of 'stay down for eight' I did just that. It also occurred to me that this short rest would also ensure that there would not be sufficient time for Fred to have another over and allowed him to come down the wicket and say with obvious feeling, 'Sorry, Trev, old son, there are many more I'd rather have hit than thee'. Then there was the occasion when he was creating a certain amount of mayhem on the edge of a swimming pool in Australia at a magnificent party given by John Mills, who was making the film *The Summer of the Seventeenth Doll* out there. I think it was Peter Richardson who suggested that it would be rather amusing if Fred took an unexpected plunge while fully clothed and I supplied the necessary push before beating a hasty and diplomatic retreat while an understandably incensed Trueman was taking punitive action on an unlucky Australian actor who was innocent but did not look it. I enjoyed making an instinctive catch off his bowling to remove Neil Harvey at Lord's. On the way to Australia we had adjoining cabins, when the amount of sleep I missed was more than compensated by the merriment it produced. Having a drink with him and listening – it is not always easy to get a word in – can by itself prove more entertaining than most T.V. shows. Crouching in the slips when he has been bowling for England. It has all been enormous fun.

No characters in the game today? You must be joking!

18

ALAN DAVIDSON

'Davoe, the Claw'

Just as the U.S.A. had its 'Quiet American', in fact as well as in fiction, I have always thought of Alan Davidson as the 'Quiet Australian'. He is a pleasant, very reliable, rather serious companion who seems destined to finish in a high executive position in the banking profession. I found him interesting to talk to, but very far removed from so many Aussie cricketers who have been keen to whoop it up given the slightest encouragement. In many respects he reminded me of the majority of star Australian tennis players, superb natural athletes, absolutely dedicated to the job, with fine physique, and rather retiring by disposition.

My first encounter with Alan Davidson, as with Richie Benaud, was in 1950, when he played for New South Wales against the M.C.C. As his side made over 500 runs in the first innings for the loss of three wickets and declared their second innings closed with two wickets down, Alan was not called upon to bat. It was a high scoring draw on a beautiful pitch and, as third seamer to Lindwall and Miller, he did not make a great impression, failing to take a wicket, but his fielding was clearly exceptional by any standard. Although he was not selected for the return match, it came as no surprise when Alan was selected to tour England under Lindsay Hassett in 1953 as one of a trio of young all-rounders of considerable potential, the others being Benaud and Ron Archer. For a first tour he did very well. In all first class matches he scored nearly 1,000 runs and captured 50 wickets at very reasonable cost, while in the field, whether close to the bat or in the deep, he was a source of menace to batsmen and delight to spectators. Although the Australians had three outstanding seam bowlers in Lindwall, Miller and Bill Johnston, Alan still forced his way into

the Test side and played in all five matches. After that series I wrote about him in a book on the series as follows:

> 'Possessing much personal charm and an unquenchable enthusiasm for the game, Alan soon made many new friends in England. He is a genuine all-rounder – a hard hitting left-hand bat, a very lively fast-medium bowler and perhaps the best all-positions fielder in a team of exceptional fieldsmen.
>
> 'In character with most other members of the side, Alan smote the ball with whole-hearted vigour so that silly mid off was never a habitable position. His bowling was accurate rather than devastating.'

In other words a fine Test all rounder had arrived; a judgement that my next tour to Australia under Sir Len Hutton and Alan's second trip to England under Ian Johnson, did nothing to alter. But what I did not anticipate was that this fine 'bits and pieces' international would, for several years, become the greatest new ball bowler of his time.

What caused this remarkable transformation? The answer is simple. Davidson mastered the art of moving the ball into the right-handed batsman from on and outside the off stump. Until that time one could play him as a normal brisk left-armer, operating from over the wicket, whose line automatically went across the right-handed batsman. Like most Australian seam bowlers, his length and direction were consistently excellent and, because he did not have to play too much top-class cricket, his pace was always sharp, nearer to fast than fast-medium. His run-up was comparatively short, about thirteen paces, and his very powerful body action was near perfection. Although not exceptionally quick in a Lindwall or a Tyson sense, he was capable of producing a distinctly unpleasant bouncer – made all the more effective because he employed it sparingly – and he hit the bat hard enough to jar the hand if you were lucky enough to remain at the crease for long.

Looking back, I should have realized how his bowling was going to improve during the final Test match in 1955. Troubled by muscle injuries, Alan had not enjoyed a particularly distinguished series against us, and only played in three of the Tests. In this final one, after we had secured the Ashes, Alan was entrusted with the role of third, instead of fourth seamer. As a result he was given the second new ball while it still had a considerable amount of shine. I happened to be batting at the time and, as usual, was pushing forward to most deliveries. Suddenly and unexpectedly, a well pitched-up ball on or around my off stump deviated sharply, swung in late and hit me painfully on my left toe. This happened on at least two more occasions in this spell and by the end of the day I was hobbling painfully and probably somewhat fortunate to be still there as I must have been very close to being out toe before wicket!

When Alan made his second visit to England any advance he might have made was prevented by circumstances over which he had no control. First, he chipped an ankle bone in the opening Test after bowling only ten overs and was unable to take any further part in the match. This injury was to keep him out of cricket for most of the remainder of the summer and he was only fit to play in the final Test. Second, the series was fought very largely on beach-like pitches which were made for finger-spinners and totally unsuited to seamers. This was the series when Jim Laker picked up 46 wickets for under ten runs apiece.

It was to be an entirely different story when, under Peter May, the M.C.C. set forth in 1958 for Australia, confident they had a side more than capable of retaining the Ashes. However, the Aussies not only gained their revenge, but Alan Davidson established himself as their recognized spearhead, a position he continued to occupy until he retired from the game. The previous winter Alan had enjoyed a highly successful tour of South Africa where he was the most penetrative attacker of the Australian bowlers, so we did realize that he had developed into a formidable adversary. Now, in the course of a tour which was clouded by the throwing controversy, it seemed to me that Alan Davidson never received the credit he deserved, as so much space was devoted to Meckiff and Rorke. Davidson did in truth bowl beautifully and, as I had been once again pressed into opening the innings, nobody had a better opportunity of appreciating his quality.

With the new ball especially, he had the ability to upset far better players than myself. I talked to Ken Barrington about Davidson's bowling on the following tour and he admitted how he had found him very hard to combat.

Alan Davidson's action was in many respects a model for bowlers, with his easy loping approach until he accelerated into his delivery stride. His braced right foot hit the ground hard and his follow-through was a delight to watch, with his left arm chasing his right across his body until finally checked by the right hip. However, what really made batting against him difficult was the way he had of nipping the odd ball back into the batsman from just outside the off stump, as well as of moving it away both in the air and off the pitch. If anyone feels that I have over-emphasized the importance of a left-arm bowler who is able to do this from over the wicket, I suggest that he examines the record of the Surrey bowler, David Sydenham. For years Sydenham was just another seamer, or steamer, of comfortable pace whom one rather looked forward to encountering. Then as a result of many hours practising in the nets, he discovered the secret of swinging the ball into the right-handed batsman and immediately began to capture a hundred wickets per year, and was even talked about as a possibility for England. On a lower plain the transformation of Sydenham from an ordinary county bowler into a hundred wickets per year man was as remarkable as that of Alan Davidson at Test level.

Davidson's last tour of England was in 1961 when he came under Richie Benaud. The Australian attack was fragile, containing only Davidson and Benaud of international calibre. As Benaud broke down with injury this put a large responsibility on Alan who responded so well that he captured twenty-three Test wickets and the Australians, greatly assisted by the English selectors, who experimented rashly and lacked consistency, were able to retain the Ashes. When England tried to put this matter right on their next trip Alan had lost a fraction of his pace, but in a high scoring period he still managed to take more wickets than any bowler on either side and these only cost twenty runs apiece. Once again, he was especially formidable with the new ball, trapping the early batsmen with the one that moved away and having them caught behind, as well as getting them lbw with the one that swung in from the off.

From 1957 until 1963 Alan Davidson claimed the finest batsmen as unwilling victims on perfect pitches. In consequence, there is a tendency to forget that he was still an all rounder in these years, even though his batting did suffer through his being called upon to do so much bowling.

He was a dangerous attacking left-hander who hit the ball uncommonly hard and the type of player who could easily transform the course of a game in a short period or, on a difficult pitch, might hit his side out of trouble. It always seemed to me that he was slightly suspect against exceptional pace, while his basic technique, especially his tendency to hit through the line without worrying overmuch about movement off the pitch, meant that he was normally giving the bowlers a chance. He never looked comfortable against Tyson, probably because he would try to smash him to the boundary, rather than pushing him there with the help of the pace of the delivery itself. However, he made the time he spent at the crease count in terms of runs scored and I was always thankful to see him returning to the pavilion.

Because of the climate and the exceptionally high standards of athleticism to be found throughout Australia, most Australians field well and a high percentage are brilliant. So, for a player to be nicknamed 'Claw' because of his ability in the field, he has to be quite exceptional. Always a fine mover, with splendid reactions and great coordination, Davidson is unquestionably one of the best all-round fieldsmen I have played against. At times it seemed he must have elastic in his arms, because the 'claw' stretched out so far. In Sydney they still talk of how in his opening games for New South Wales, before anyone had heard of him, he made a regular habit of running out the opposition by means of his deceptive speed over the ground combined with an accurate throw of which Colin Bland would not be ashamed.

The life of a quick bowler in first class cricket is hard and inevitably all Test men break down from time to time with injuries of varying importance. Alan Davidson, despite his splendid physique, was almost a record holder in this department, indeed his colleagues were amazed if he was *not* suffering from some minor ailment or other; yet few ever affected his performance with ball, bat, or in the field. There once was talk of running a sweep on the time Alan spent on the massage table; however, the fact remains that Alan – with a touch of fibrositis in his left shoulder, a slight strain in the back, and a little niggle in the ankle – continued to take wickets, which, after all, is by far the best medicine for dressing-room injuries.

It was a tonic on which Alan Davidson – a real artist with a new ball, a dangerous striker with the bat, and a superb fieldsman – positively thrived.

F

19

TONY LOCK

'Sir Beau'

The cricketing saga of Tony Lock is unique, for it has had three distinct phases. He started his career for Surrey as an orthodox slow left-hander and continued in this fashion for several seasons. Then he spent one winter in an indoor school where a low roof prevented anyone flighting a ball and ensured a flat trajectory. When he re-emerged next summer he had completely amended his style and very quickly became one of the most lethal spinners this country has seen.

Lock altered his action for the third and final time when he became caught up in the throwing controversy which broke out during the 1957–8 M.C.C. tour of Australia. Tony was severely shaken by some movie-pictures and immediately decided to take the steps necessary to clear himself of the probable charge of throwing. He was then at the very height of his powers – and an automatic Test selection, at least in England – so that to abandon his whole technique almost overnight took a considerable amount of courage, which is, perhaps, his outstanding characteristic. The fact that he not only reshaped his action and adopted a new style, but managed again to reach the top of his profession and be picked for England, is a tribute to his dedication, professionalism, and his deep love for cricket. In addition no cricketer has ever played for Surrey and England, emigrated and played state cricket in Australia and finally played regular county cricket in the English summer and state cricket in the Australian summer, let alone captaining both his teams, Leicestershire and Western Australia. He is also the first Englishman to be summoned from Australia to join an M.C.C. team in the West Indies.

It is interesting, however, that Tony Lock was not completely convinced that he had transgressed the law in his middle phase

until one evening when he was having dinner with Sir Don Bradman in Australia. After the meal the Don showed him a 16 mm.
film of his bowling in the 1960 series against the Australians with
his present action and then some shots of when he had operated
at medium pace with a left arm that straightened, with more than
a suspicion of a jerk.

In his final phase Lock was no longer quite the same devastating force as in his middle period, at least in England, but there
is still no better left-arm spinner in the country. On the other
hand, abroad, the transition to his present method eventually
proved beneficial and he became a more effective bowler. This
has been shown by his performances for Western Australia. He
has learned to rely more upon guile, flight and variation which
pay on true, covered pitches. Only recently he broke the post-
war record for the highest number of victims in a season of
Sheffield Shield cricket.

Tony Lock is very much a cricketer's cricketer. His worth to
any side cannot merely be measured in terms of the wickets he
takes, the runs he makes, and the catches he holds. He has an
aggressiveness and determination which is infectious, while he is
never prepared to surrender, as he showed so plainly in his last
wicket stand with Pocock in the fifth Test at Georgetown in 1968.

As a bowler he never wants to come off and will not allow a
matter of a raw or bleeding spinning finger to interfere with the
job in hand. As a batsman, despite certain obvious limitations, he
is always prepared to sell his life dearly, or to cut and carve according to the dictates of the situation. One of my favourite sights in
cricket is to see 'Sir Beau' striding nonchalantly to the crease in
an effort to save the game. He is a great rearguard specialist and
this is the type of situation he adores, although meandering out
to the wicket, accompanied by shouts from the crowd, would be
a rather more accurate description than striding. At the crease
he will take a leisurely guard, carefully investigate any defects
in the pitch, real or imaginary, survey the disposition of the enemy
troops, and finally is prepared to do battle.

One of the few times I have seen 'Sir Beau' bewildered and bemused was against South Africa on a rough wicket at Pretoria.

We were struggling to avoid defeat when Tony joined me at the crease. Just before the close the South African captain, Jackie McGlew, departed from the field without telling us his intentions. It subsequently transpired that he was claiming the extra half hour. With another day left this would have been standard practice in England, but I was unaware that this particular rule applied in matches in South Africa against the tourists. When the clock signalled close of play there was still no sign of McGlew, who was looking through the local rules. Seeing no point in working overtime and running the risk of losing another wicket, I decided to depart. The result was that there was the rather unusual sight of two batsmen marching pavilion-wards – Tony was about twenty yards behind me – while the umpires and the fielding side remained uncertain what to do. By the time the matter had been settled I had showered and there was only five minutes of the extra half hour left.

The theatrical touch, which is a feature of everything Tony does, is especially noticeable in his fielding. He has been one of the very best, and certainly one of the most spectacular of short legs. He is seldom content merely to bring off a breath-taking catch, but likes to throw in a dive and a couple of somersaults for good measure. I remember him taking a wonderful catch off his own bowling in a Test match against the Australians and finishing up by rolling over and over down towards the unfortunate batsman. As a short leg Tony is equally at home to either spin or speed and is absolutely fearless. He has evolved his own technique and is not content to stand motionless and crouching. He edges forward as the ball is being delivered and this, combined with his quick reflexes and ability to anticipate, have helped him to make catches, especially with his left hand, that many players would not even consider half chances. Although he became recognized as a specialist short leg he is in fact a first class fielder anywhere. His throwing is particularly deadly – as one cynic once suggested, he had plenty of practice !

In August 1949, at Southend, Surrey defeated Essex by an innings, an uncomfortable but certainly not unique event. However, this match had a certain significance for me, because it gave me

my first view of Tony Lock. At the time nobody could have foreseen that the slow, graceful left-hander with the almost classical
style, possessing plenty of hair and using the air, would develop
eventually into a balding, solidly constructed, medium-pace
spinner with a flat trajectory, who in certain conditions was
virtually unplayable. Looking back, it is interesting to recall that
when Essex started to crumple on a wearing pitch on our second
innings, Lock was not even called upon, indeed he made rather
more impression as an irritating 'tail-end' batsman than as a
bowler.

In the light of later events it is worth recording what Wisden
had to say about him after he had established himself in the Surrey
side of 1951 : 'Lock, the young left-arm bowler, maintained his
promise, but unless he imparts more spin to his leg-break will not
reach the pinnacle'. In those days he had to rely for his wickets
largely upon a teasing flight and a reasonable command of length.
He was relatively speaking more effective on good wickets when
he aimed to entice the batsmen to drive him through a packed
off side field. This provided some delightful cricket for spectators,
but only a limited number of victims for the bowler himself.

The transformation of Tony Lock from just another slow left-
arm spinner into a destroyer of opposing batsmen was remarkable in many ways. Strictly speaking, it should never have been
allowed and could never have occurred if the umpires and the
authorities of those days had been as bent-arm conscious as they
now are. At the beginning of that season, when Tony introduced
his new style of bowling for the first time, two of his colleagues
were strolling by the nets and saw him in action. They were
amazed and one remarked to the other, 'Well, if he can get away
with it, good luck to him !'

Why was everyone, or nearly everyone, so blind? Why didn't
the Surrey committee, which contains some extremely distinguished cricketers, notice anything strange? I suppose the answer
was that people tend to see what they want to see. Moreover, the
metamorphosis of Tony Lock from just an ordinary slow left-
hander to a deadly medium-paced spinner ought to have caused
more than an occasional raised eyebrow and a hostile demonstra-

tion when one umpire, Fred Price, had the sense to call him in a county match.

Until the arrival of the 'new-look' Lock it was Jim Laker who had done most of the damage for Surrey on worn pitches, but it was a different story once Tony changed his technique. From that moment Surrey had the best pair of spinners in the country, and indeed the world. On any wicket in England they were formidable and if there was something in the pitch they were deadly. Often The Oval of those days appeared to have been made especially for these two, so that visiting batsmen tended to think:

> Ashes to ashes and dust to dust
> If Laker doesn't get me 'Locky' must.

Tony was at his most valuable on a really slow pitch which took spin. In these circumstances a good batsman had time to adjust his shots against the normal slow bowler, but Tony's exceptional pace through the air did not allow him to do this. It is all very well to advocate using one's feet against spinners, but against Lock, unless one was prepared to go down the track before the ball was delivered, it was not possible. I remember standing in the slips with David Sheppard as Lock sliced his way through the powerful West Indian batting in the fifth Test at The Oval in 1957. I posed the following question to David: 'How do you play a left-hand medium-pace bowler who keeps pitching leg stump and fizzing over the top of the off?' Neither of us could supply the answer, and nor could the West Indians.

Though I always queried the legality of Tony's action, except when I was on the same side, I realized that I was very much in the minority and, appreciating this, I decided to look for a bent-arm spinner for Essex. If Surrey and England could employ one without concern, why should not my own county?

Overseas Tony's action normally caused less comment, because the cricketers generally were prepared to tolerate a bent arm. Australia certainly had its share of dart players long before the controversy while Tony's bowling arm was less crooked than, say, Ian Johnson's!

Tony was at his most successful abroad in India and Pakistan, and especially on the mat, but in other countries he did not produce exceptional figures. The main reason for this was that he was not prepared or wise enough at that stage of his career, to try to change his basic technique. Even Tony could not pitch leg and hit off in Australia, South Africa and the West Indies, he still attempted the impossible so that batsmen tended to treat him as a medium pacer rather than a spinner.

Although the legitimacy of Tony's action was generally accepted, he had one particular delivery, the quick one, which caused controversy wherever he went. His fast ball was easily the fastest I have ever encountered and was rightly viewed with consternation by all. When the M.C.C. were in the West Indies the Jamaican Board of Control brought back by public subscription the great old master, George Headley, to play against us. George came in to bat and before he had become acclimatized Tony unleashed his 'quickie'. It was genuinely fast and George was still lifting his bat as the wicket was struck. In another match Tony sent a batsman's stumps flying, something which even Fred Trueman, flat out, found difficulty in doing. On this occasion the square leg umpire quite correctly called him for throwing. Understandably he was rather late and both stumps were on the ground by the time he had shouted. After that experience Lock refrained from using it again on that tour, but he was still allowed to employ it in England. I can recall him shooting out Doug Insole in the Champion County v. The Rest match. After the wicket had been hit Doug remained long enough to enquire of the umpire whether he had been bowled or run out and I followed him to the crease. As Tony hustled up to bowl I emitted a reasonable facsimile of a no-ball shout. This piece of gamesmanship upset Tony, always a volatile person, and consequently made batting for me a little easier on that occasion. After the close Arthur Macintyre, one of the best wicket-keepers and one of the nicest people in the game, complained that, though my action had its humorous side, it could affect Tony's livelihood – which allowed me to point out that batsmen also had to live.

I have had the pleasure of touring with Tony on a number of occasions and we quickly discovered that we possessed two important things in common, a passion for Westerns and a love of good food. I have lost count of the number of times that Tony and I have watched the good sheriff out-draw and out-shoot the 'baddie'. We have eaten with gourmet satisfaction some outstanding meals in many different parts of the world with the result that both of us have considerably expanded our girths.

Watching Tony Lock prepare to take the field is fascinating. Every conceivable portion of his anatomy is encased in bandages, plasters and supports, so that he resembles a mummy and with reason one wonders how he is going to live through the remainder of the day, let alone play cricket.

It is noticeable how many batsmen who occupy the later places in the order are suspect against excessive pace, and often show their unhappiness by a retreat towards the square leg umpire. This is a criticism which certainly could never be levelled at Tony who has always been more than prepared to stand up to anything and anybody. He revels in a fight. He is, of course, rather too useful with the bat to be labelled a 'tail-ender' and comes into the awkward category of bowlers who can score runs. If he had been brought up abroad, and had not had to play cricket six and often seven days per week, he would in all probability have been an all-rounder. As it is he is quite capable of taking thirty or forty runs off a top-class attack when the pressure is on. He is an unmistakable figure at the crease, with his rather ugly crouching stance and a pair of pads that never seem to fit properly; and he can hit surprisingly hard, his best stroke being the cut.

In the 1960s Tony decided to emigrate to Australia and became the first Englishman (since the war) to play regular first class cricket there. In addition to representing Western Australia with considerable success he also proved himself to be a fine and enthusiastic coach. It seemed that England, outside the leagues, had seen the last of this remarkable person until Leicester, who were struggling near the foot of the table, persuaded him to come to their aid. This has proved an especially wise investment and he now captains his adopted county with the skill and the driving enthusiasm which is so typical. These days a wicket taken by a Leicester bowler is the signal for an effusive demonstration by their skipper which would not be out of place in a Cup Final. Tactically Tony is sound and he has been able to mould together a number of talented individuals into a decidedly useful combination which finished second equal in the Championship table. He is unquestionably one of the outstanding characters of the game, while his keenness and dedication are a watchword. He manages to impart far more feeling, effort and desperation into one appeal than many cricketers are able to give to their actual bowling.

20

GODFREY EVANS

The Cheeky Chappie

To me Godfrey Evans will always be the Max Miller of the cricket scene, the original 'Cheeky Chappie'. His breezy, bouncy character enabled him to say and do things which would have been unacceptable from anyone else. Occasionally, very occasionally, this might cause offence or be misinterpreted and I can recall a certain rather dignified governor with a military background not entirely appreciating Godfrey's suggestion – almost a demand – for cigars and champagne. However, rebuffs of this nature were rare and made no impression on Godfrey, who sometimes seems to have been born in the wrong century. His personality is almost too rich and vivid for the somewhat uniform age in which we live. He would have made a superb, rumbustious Viking.

Godfrey Evans was, quite simply, the finest wicket-keeper I have seen. At his very best he was capable of making catches and stumpings which no other man would have considered chances. An instance of this occurred in the Test trial at Bradford when Jim Laker ran riot to the tune of eight wickets for two runs. Don Kenyon moved back to a ball that turned and lifted unpleasantly. He played it down and Godfrey managed to catch it one-handed, a full length *in front* of the batsman and equally astonished short legs. I was one of these and had not even moved! On another occasion during a Scarborough Festival match, Billy Sutcliffe glanced a delivery from Alec Bedser wide, off the full face of the bat. Godfrey, as usual standing up to Alec, anticipated, took off and caught the ball one-handed while literally horizontal.

Like so many great players, Godfrey thrived on the big occasion, and it is fair to say that he was normally a better keeper for England than for Kent. For it is not possible to turn in superlative performances every day of the week as a wicket-keeper.

The one
and only
"GODDERS"

The central figure in the field must always be the man behind the stumps. Not only does he have the opportunity to make more catches than anyone else, but he delivers the *coup de grâce* in the majority of run outs, and he is also responsible for the stumpings. He can transform the whole appearance of the fielding side, camouflaging the poorer turns and adding colour to the proceedings. He is the hub around which the remainder of the team revolves and Godfrey revelled in all this. His bubbling enthusiasm also did much to keep his team going, especially towards the end of a long, hot, unsuccessful day in the field. He was a tonic with his 'We only need two more wickets tonight and we're through them', even though the score at that particular juncture was 330 for 2!

I have played over fifty Test matches with Godfrey Evans and consider the 1950–1 series in Australia his most outstanding. I cannot remember him putting down a catch, or missing a single stumping in five Test matches, while in addition he made a number of 'impossible' catches, especially off Alec Bedser. Godfrey's keeping helped Alec Bedser enormously, and one catch full length down the leg side which dismissed a plainly hypnotized Neil Harvey from a glance off the face of the bat, will always be with me.

It is extremely difficult to pinpoint Godfrey's most outstanding match, but I would choose the fifth Test against the South Africans at Port Elizabeth on a pitch which made the 'beach' at Old Trafford where the Australians were 'Lakered' appear reasonable by comparison. At least two balls per over shot straight along the ground and from the point of view of the wicket-keeper it would be difficult to imagine worse conditions. However, Godfrey never put a glove wrong and I remember remarking to Peter Richardson as we came off the field at the end of play that the feature of that game for me was unquestionably Godfrey behind the stumps. He had not been merely good, he had been superb.

What was the secret of his success? Apart from sheer ability and a superb eye, it was very largely a matter of vitality. Many people can be brilliant for a short period of time, but it takes a very exceptional person to be just as full of life and just as spectacular an hour before the close of play on a really hot day at

Adelaide after five successive sessions in the field. The fact that Godfrey Evans was a born entertainer who welcomed the limelight, and possessed a flair for the spectacular and the audacious, not only made him a universal favourite with spectators; it acted also as a spur to the fielders to maintain the standard he set himself.

In two respects Godfrey was fortunate. He was able to take a swift nap and awake refreshed under the most difficult circumstances. On numerous occasions I have seen him come in at lunchtime, have a drink and then curl up and go to sleep, completely oblivious to the noise of a dressing-room. The other reason underlying his success was his ability to dismiss instantly from his mind any mistake he might make. Many wicket-keepers spend five minutes apologizing for a dropped catch and the rest of the day bemoaning that particular blunder. This may be understandable, but it does not help when the next chance comes along.

Very occasionally he did have a bad day. His worst was at Leeds in 1948 against the Australians, when they turned defeat into victory with a large second innings score on a worn wicket as chance after chance went down. From a purely personal angle I shall remember him dropping Neil Harvey at Manchester. Neil had just come to the crease and managed to get an outside edge. It travelled sweetly to Godfrey, standing back, who was throwing it and appealing when down it went. Throughout Neil's hundred I was haunted by that moment, but not Godfrey.

Godfrey has always been a great lover of parties and should one tend to drag he was just the person to instil that extra zip. In the past the M.C.C. touring team used to travel out by ship and one of the highlights of the voyage was the fancy dress dance. At these times Godfrey was at his best and made a magnificent and vivacious Carmen Miranda. On race night he would set up as an unorthodox, quick-talking, very noisy, colourfully attired bookmaker in opposition to the ship's Tote. His performances became almost legendary. Even his partners in his book-making enterprises were apt, unless not completely sober, to be more than a little worried by the starting prices he offered during dinner, but he was usually lucky. Indeed he is a genuine punter, happy to celebrate a win, but never complaining when he loses; and he subscribes to the view that there is all the more call for champagne after the latter than the former!

As a character Godfrey is in fact like a good vintage champagne, full of verve, sparkle, and life, except for the odd bottle which is very flat. On these rare occasions his depression, though short, is liable to be deep. However, one of his most engaging traits is his instinctive generosity. He is invariably the first to buy a round and never counts the cost. Perhaps this, combined with his inborn impetuosity, is why some of his commercial ventures have failed to turn out as successfully as he hoped. There are many times when it is essential to wait in business, but waiting is foreign to Godfrey's temperament. He always wanted to make the first million within six months, and was not prepared to wait a year.

Godfrey was such an outstanding wicket-keeper that his ability as a batsman is often forgotten. He was not brilliant, but he was a useful performer at international level and capable of making over a thousand runs a year in County Cricket if he really concentrated. In this connection he had his best season for Kent with the bat when somebody had a sizable bet on his not reaching an aggregate of four figures. However, in domestic cricket he was usually content with a bright and breezy knock which did not last too long. He knew that had he really concentrated in this department it could have affected the standard of his keeping. He enjoyed his batting and so did the spectators.

I was probably directly involved in more of his important Test innings than anyone else. A high percentage of our partnerships were rearguard actions, when our respective techniques blended naturally, and I certainly loved to have him at the other end. He was ever an optimist and would strut up to me at the start and say, 'Now then, Trevor, what's been going on out here? We'll knock these runs off tonight.' The fact that only three wickets remained and we needed another 300 runs made no difference. Although he had an epic stand with Denis Compton at Sydney in the 1946–7 tour when he did not score a run for a very long time, Godfrey was at his best in a swashbuckling attacking role, for his defence was never sound. He liked to hit hard and often – in addition to the normal strokes he became particularly adept at a shovel shot with which he used to scoop the ball out towards mid-wicket, using plenty of right hand – and to scamper enthusiastically between the wickets. His running was a tonic to the spectators, the fieldsmen, and certainly not least to his partner. He introduced a note of genuine comedy, but never forgot the importance of the stolen single or the advantage to be gained by backing up.

The most significant partnership I had with Godfrey was against the West Indies in 1950 at Old Trafford. The pitch was one of the worst I have ever encountered, a broken beach on which Eric Hollies made the odd delivery rear shoulder high, as well as turn, and the English batting collapsed against the spin combination of Ramadhin and Valentine. When the 'Cheeky Chappie' joined me we were in serious trouble with all the accredited players back in the pavilion and less than 100 runs on the board. Godfrey was completely undeterred. He cut and carved with such impunity that he not only scored a remarkable century, but together we managed to make the record stand for that particular wicket. Before the end the West Indians were not sure where to bowl. England consequently regained command and went on to record our one victory of the series.

The most satisfying boundary Godfrey Evans ever struck was against the Australians at Adelaide. With only four runs required to win the game and the Ashes I foolishly lost my wicket. In he went, smote the ball to the mid-wicket pickets, and the champagne was waiting for him by the time he returned to the pavilion.

Soon after the Selectors had decided to find a successor for him in the England team, Godfrey decided to retire from the first class game. He needed the spur of international matches to hold his interest. My one regret was that he did not become the first person to win a hundred caps. However, in the summer of 1967, although he had not kept in a county game for years, Kent persuaded him to come to their aid when Alan Knott was picked to represent England for the first time and they were due to meet

Yorkshire. Needless to say, Godfrey could not resist such a challenge and in the circumstances gave an incredible performance.

Had this situation not arisen I should have had the honour of captaining Godfrey on what he intended to be his farewell performance. This was for the International Cavaliers against Barbados in the West Indies. It was the final match of a happy tour. Unfortunately we were by then so badly hit by injuries that we could not raise a fully fit side. In order that the game should not peter out into a draw I declared, leaving our opponents a total to make against the clock, although my attack had by that time been reduced to only two recognized bowlers. Godfrey, despite a painful septic knee, insisted on keeping wicket and proceeded to pull out all the stops. For some two and a half hours the crowd saw the one and only 'Godders' in action. Increasing age and girth could not disguise the fact that here was a great personality and a superb craftsman, the like of which we are unlikely to see again.

21

KEITH MILLER
'Nugget'

The belief is still current in England that Australian males are tall, lean, tanned and tough, narrow at the waist and broad of shoulder. There is no more than a grain of truth in this generalization, but Keith Miller so epitomized their dream Australian that the British public took him to their hearts, even though many jeered when he subjected the English batsmen to an overdose of bouncers – when only one side, as in 1948, is capable of providing bumpers, supporters of the other side are always inclined to be over-sensitive. Even Miller's nickname of 'Nugget' was in keeping with the 'golden boy' from 'Down Under'. It was not only his outstanding physique and sheer cricketing ability that appealed, but that he did everything with so much ease and natural grace. In addition he possessed, like great actors, a presence, so that even his mannerisms, as when he impatiently tossed back his mane of hair, added to his stature.

My first encounter with Keith Miller was in a wartime match at Hove. Miller arrived at the ground, characteristically on the late side, wearing the dark blue uniform of the R.A.A.F. He carried all the cricket gear he possessed with him, a shirt nonchalantly slung over his shoulders, and a well worn pair of boots in his hand. Someone lent him some trousers and he did not bother about socks. In those days he had already made a considerable impression as an attacking batsman, but his bowling was an unknown quantity.

The Navy, for whom I was playing, batted first and against some rather friendly bowling I put together a reasonable score. Suddenly the opposing captain in desperation tossed the ball to Keith and asked him to turn his arm over. He ambled back a few perfunctory paces and I still do not know who was more surprised, the wicket-keeper – who was standing up – or myself, when the ball shot by the stumps for four byes before either of us had really moved. Miller was the fastest fifth-change bowler I have ever had the misfortune to encounter!

In 1948 Keith returned to England as a key member of Donald Bradman's all-conquering team. At the time I was in the Cambridge XI which the tourists crushed by an innings and about 50 runs, having first declared for the loss of only four wickets. Keith did not have a knock, although another large score would have put him well on the way to a thousand runs in May, but he did a considerable amount of damage with the ball, including a direct hit on my head when I ducked into a bouncer. This brought forth a rumbustious appeal for lbw, which was disallowed.

The Australians' very next match was against Essex. This turned out to be little less than a massacre with the Australians amassing some 721 runs in a day at a methodical 240-odd runs per session. Keith was promoted to No. 4, but by the time he reached the wicket, the score was well over 300. This type of situation had no appeal for him and he allowed himself to be bowled first ball. As the lucky bowler I was both delighted and somewhat bewildered to see the stumps disappearing out of the ground. He was certainly never as charitable to me again. Don Bradman was batting at the other end and remarked that 'he'll learn'. Keith's somewhat theatrical gesture was something the Don found difficult to fathom, because it was so foreign to his own outlook.

I next met Miller during the 1950–1 M.C.C. tour to Australia and from then on we bowled and batted against each other through four hard-fought series. During this time it was often reported that a feud existed between us. This was not true – indeed I have always greatly admired Keith – but our differences in character and outlook served to make the rumour credible. Keith was a natural gambler; I have a cautious streak. He possessed so many talents that he could afford on occasions to squander them; I have always had to play within my limitations. He tended to be impatient and romantic, I patient and utilitarian. In many respects, indeed, this was another example of Cavalier v. Roundhead. It was also true that I sometimes annoyed Keith,

"Nugget"

which gave me a perverse pleasure. I remember being hit by a bouncer from him at Leeds. Understandably he was getting somewhat irritated by the continual forward prod. He followed up this bouncer with a fast head-high full toss from which I managed to take the necessary evasive action. I have never minded bouncers, but I objected to 'beamers'; so I waited until he was about to deliver the next ball, walked away, removed my gloves and examined the finger which had been struck by the bumper.

When he was batting it was also possible, and sometimes profitable, to provoke him into making a rash stroke by deliberately shutting up the game. He did not like being restricted. It was foreign to his nature, and his predictable reaction was to lash out, without always weighing up the odds. These tactics certainly brought about his downfall on more than one occasion.

However, for all our differences we had one common characteristic : both of us have always inclined towards wayward individualism.

How good a cricketer was Keith Miller? He was quite simply the finest and the most spectacular all-rounder of his time; indeed there can have been few, if any, better in the history of the game until the arrival of Gary Sobers. It was not merely the runs he scored, the wickets he captured, or the catches he took that made him great, it was the way these were achieved that stamped him as a cricket immortal.

As a batsman, Keith, with his pronounced initial forward movement, was rather more English than Australian in technique. In these circumstances it is rather surprising that he was not more at home against the turning ball. Watching him lunge and shuffle, while trying to fathom out the mysteries of Jim Laker on a bad wicket, it was difficult to appreciate that he could also be one of the outstanding stroke players in the world. As one would expect from his high back lift and grip, he was an exceptionally good and powerful driver and, like so many Australians, a brilliant cutter. He was rather too much of a forward lunger to be a good hooker of fast bowling, and this was also a handicap against the exceptional pace of someone like Frank Tyson. However, his straight bat hitting off both the front and back foot was of such exceptional quality that it reminded the older generation of the golden age. At Adelaide, which has a very long straight boundary, I remember him hitting two sixes over the sight screen. One was struck with the weight on the leading foot, and the other on the back foot. Both blows had an enormous carry and I always felt he was one of the very few people who might have reached Tags Island at East Molesey cricket ground. In a one-day friendly match the Australians took part in there in 1953, he certainly came close, although the biggest hit was registered by Ray Lindwall.

Keith was potentially a better batsman in his early days, but later the amount of bowling he was called upon to do prevented him reaching the heights he might have achieved. I would not rate him as the greatest fast bowler I have faced, but he was certainly the most mercurial, unpredictable and, in certain circumstances, the most devastating. His approach was short and his body action superb. He is the only quick bowler I have ever batted against who has dropped the ball in his run up, retrieved it in one effortless movement, and carried on bowling as if nothing unusual had occurred. He was often at his most lethal just when the opposition appeared to be taking control. On a number of occasions England would appear to be nicely placed. Then midway through a hot afternoon's session Keith would come on with an old ball on a placid pitch and transform the course of the match in a few inspired overs.

The problems of batting against Miller were many. He was genuinely fast, while his high arm action, combined with his height, enabled him to achieve considerable lift from only just short of a length. At times he moved the ball in the air, but, unlike Ray Lindwall, he was more of a seam than a swing bowler. Sometimes he would become bored with bowling, looking upon it as an unwelcome and monotonous chore; indeed it seemed to me that he gained less pleasure from it than any other great bowler. On these occasions he was just as likely to unleash a barrage of bumpers, or a googly, or a round-arm slinger.

Of all his many bowling feats against England, including those ten wickets in the match at Lord's in 1956, I am not sure that his opening spell in our second innings at Adelaide in 1954–5 was not perhaps his finest. England only required 94 runs to win not only the match, but the Ashes. It all seemed simple as the pitch itself was slow and easy, but we failed to take into account Miller who, in the course of twenty balls, removed Hutton, Edrich and Cowdrey and yet again we were struggling.

Keith Miller was an instinctive fieldsman with exceptional reactions. He was certainly the most relaxed and casual slip I have seen, but he was one of the most brilliant. He would be standing upright, hands behind his back, discussing something really important like the winner of the next race, when he would suddenly swoop to bring off a diving catch inches from the ground. It has often been said that a slip should not anticipate, but Keith was a law unto himself. I can still clearly remember Cyril Washbrook cutting a long hop from Ian Johnson, only to find himself caught full length by Keith who had moved from slip to gulley.

Keith Miller was never entrusted with the Australian captaincy and that may well have been a big mistake. A natural rebel, he has never been a great respecter of persons and, as I have indicated, his outlook has usually differed vastly from that of Sir Donald Bradman, the most important figure since he retired in Australian cricket administration. In my opinion, Keith Miller would have responded to the responsibility and might well have become an outstanding skipper. I certainly would have liked to play under him.

22

RICHIE BENAUD

All-Rounder Extraordinaire

Initially I suppose, it was my sub-conscious which made me regard Richie with suspicion. After all, what was a straightforward looking Australian doing with a name like Benaud? It had a subtle continental flavour, far removed from basic Bondi. It would have suited a cardinal, or perhaps a mediaeval ambassador, and made me feel that behind an extremely prepossessing exterior he must be hatching some Machiavellian plot.

Our first encounter did nothing to eradicate this impression because he bowled me for nine, as I groped pathetically down the wrong line. This was during the 1950–1 M.C.C. tour when Benaud was struggling to command a regular place in an exceptionally strong New South Wales combination. On that occasion I was his sole victim on a beautiful pitch. He was not required to bat as his team amassed over 500 runs for the loss of only three wickets, and it was not until he came to England under Lindsay Hassett in 1953 that I really began to appreciate his all-round ability.

The 1953 series was notable, not only because the Ashes at long last returned to England, but because it was very even and remained undecided until the final Test. For the up-and-coming Benaud it was not an especially successful tour. He was an occasional member of the Test side, ran into a horrible patch with the bat and his two Test victims cost 87 runs each. Only on the field was he consistently brilliant. The catch he made to dismiss Colin Cowdrey at Lord's was unforgettable. Panther-like he gobbled up a full-blooded cut off the middle of the bat while standing very close in the gulley. Nevertheless there were clear indications that Richie would cause England a great deal of trouble in the years that lay ahead. At Scarborough, for example, he made 135 out of 209 in 110 minutes with one of the most exhilarating exhibitions of power-batting ever seen in the Festival; and in its long history this ground has certainly witnessed more gay abandon and batting mayhem than most. Benaud was especially severe on Roy Tattersall whom he repeatedly stroked for six straight back over his head. The force behind his driving on the up was phenomenal, so that the ball bounced back in a most spectacular way off the walls into the back gardens of the houses that overlook the arena.

Unlike the majority of overseas visitors, Richie was primarily a forward player. He possessed a top-of-the-handle grip and a high flowing backlift which was an asset when driving, but sometimes proved his undoing when confronted by exceptional speed, like that of Frank Tyson. He was an attractive player to watch, who was always more effective when he was able to attack because this suited his temperament and because his defensive technique was never more than 'adequate'. On a pitch where the ball moved about, his best chance of making runs was to chance his arm.

When England, under Sir Len Hutton, retained the Ashes in 1954–5, Richie became a permanent member of the Australian side, which was rather surprising as his performances were unexceptional with both bat and ball. This tended to give substance to a popular theory that, though it was hard to become a member of the Australian team, it was even more difficult to lose one's place, once having been accepted as a regular. This certainly does not apply to English cricket where change for change's sake seems an all-too-frequent occurrence. In the long run, the selectors' perseverance with Benaud paid off handsomely, because gradually he developed into a world class all-rounder as well as eventually becoming an outstanding captain.

It was to be expected that Richie would take some time to reach his full potential. This is normal with the majority of slow bowlers, and especially with wrist-spinners, who must expect a long, hard and often frustrating apprenticeship. Those that come through it normally do not reach their peak until their thirties and this was certainly the case with Benaud. On his first trip to England, he was very much a novice leg-spinner. Essex for instance, played the Australians at Southend on a ground which had been flooded

Spinner of Leg breaks and Words.

Test Match

RICHIE BENAUD
News of the World

Roy ULLYETT.

by the sea during the previous winter. The outcome was a pitch which crumbled badly after the first day. The other Australian leg-break bowler, Doug Ring, turned the ball square, but Richie was unable to exploit the conditions, in fact he hardly made it deviate, because he was over-spinning. Even when he returned to England in 1956, he still had much to learn. England on this occasion held on to the Ashes, largely because we won the toss when it counted most, and because the Surrey spin combination of Laker and Lock was able to make the best use of wickets that were ideal for finger-spinners. In sharp contrast the two Australian slow bowlers, Benaud and Ian Johnson, could only manage fourteen wickets between them at a prohibitive cost, to Laker's 46 and Lock's 15.

In the case of Johnson the reason for his lack of success was that he was too slow through the air to exploit a turning wicket to the full in England. He spun the ball, but relied far more on flight than the average English finger-spinner, who tends to dig the ball in flat rather than giving it air. Relatively speaking, Ian was far more dangerous on the hard, fast, true pitches of Australia. In these conditions he could still achieve a modicum of break plus some bounce, while here his over-spun off break did drift disconcertingly away from the batsman. He was especially effective against those players who were not prepared to use their feet, but I doubt whether his corkscrew action would have been favourably regarded by present umpires. Benaud bowled his leg-breaks quickly, but on crumbling pitches in England the wrist-spinner is seldom as effective as the accurate finger-spinner, although Bruce Dooland and Eric Hollies were rare exceptions to this generalization. It must also be remembered that at the time Richie had not reached his peak, he was very much the artisan rather than the artist.

On his final trip to England in 1961, Benaud was regarded as the best wrist-spinner in the world which by this time was a very fair assessment of his worth. Unfortunately, he broke down at the outset of the tour with an inflamed tendon so that we never were able to estimate fairly how well he might have bowled in this country which, since the war, has been so much more receptive to seam and finger spin than all other forms of attack. Could he, for example, have repeated the triumphs of Grimmett and O'Reilly in the thirties? Personally, I have my doubts. Nevertheless, despite his injury he enjoyed his best Test series as a bowler in England, collecting fifteen wickets at well over thirty apiece. It is interesting also to note that six of these were taken in the second innings at Old Trafford when the English batsmen, in their effort to force a victory, allowed themselves to forget the elementary principle of playing a leg-spinner bowling into the rough from around the wicket, which is to use the pads as a second line of defence.

To appreciate Richie's calibre as a leg-break bowler, I think it was necessary to play against him on good fast pitches. These were where he had learnt his craft and on which he was at his most formidable. One of the many problems, for instance, that he provided was the way he made the odd delivery bounce. On numerous occasions the batsman would go to cut a near long-hop only for it to pop and he would find himself caught at the wicket off the top edge.

Although Richie was never a prodigious spinner, his length was good, exceptionally so, and he had a dangerous googly, though because of his high, almost classical action, I found it easier to pick than from a bowler who is more round-arm. However, his body action certainly did assist him to make the ball dip in flight, and this was especially true of his top spinner. Often he would bring about the dismissal of a batsman who attempted to drive what appeared to be a half-volley only to find that it had pitched just a shade shorter. Personally, I found his 'flipper' his most difficult delivery. He concealed it with great skill and made it hurry off the pitch in such a way that a batsman would still be completing his stroke when rapped on the pads. He completely deceived me with this ball at Sydney in 1958, and I shall never know why the umpire did not give me lbw. He bowled exceptionally well throughout this series when he used himself in a supporting role to the main threat of pace. In these circumstances, I was pleased that Richie only had my scalp on one occasion, when he had me caught on the square leg boundary, a somewhat unlikely death!

Just as Richie's bowling was more telling outside England, so was his batting. He thrived on a fast pitch and a true bounce without too much deviation off the seam. He was never a consistent player, but he had the ability to produce a match-winning innings liable to transform the whole character of the game in a relatively short period of time, while he could 'murder' tired bowling. His first Test century came in only seventy-eight minutes when he flayed a wilting West Indian attack to all parts of Kingston. However, it is fair to say that he did not make as many runs against England as he should have done; our attack over this period was usually strong and the cricket so tight that it did not favour the dashing stroke player.

Benaud was one of the most astute and popular captains of Australia. He was a born ambassador and a natural leader with a well developed tactical appreciation of the game. This flair was much in evidence when he led the Australians in England in 1961. He had under his command a very ordinary combination which contained only two bowlers of international calibre, Alan Davidson and himself. Despite his own effectiveness being greatly reduced through injury, he managed to return with the Ashes by exploiting to the full the many blunders made by England both on the field and in the selection room. It was a masterly exhibition of how to make the best use of limited material.

One of the more intriguing facets of his captaincy was the way he was able to camouflage a hard practical outlook beneath a cloak of what appeared on the surface to be extreme generosity. Like any captain of worth, he was loath to give the opposition anything, but he had the gift of appearing gay, dashing, and quixotic. He would have made a superb P.R.O. or politician. Since he was by profession a journalist, he appreciated far more than most the importance of having a good 'image'. Knowing the power of the press, he went out of his way to assist journalists. No captain surely has held quite so many informal press conferences, and, because he had an easy manner and knew what they wanted from him, there were usually successful. Perhaps he occasionally overdid things – a rather cynical cricket writer once remarked 'it won't be long before he's writing the series for us as well' – nevertheless, his objective approach to the press was infinitely better than the treatment they so often receive from cricket authorities who tend, sometimes understandably perhaps, to regard journalists with suspicion.

Sir Frank Worrell was another captain who enjoyed good press relations so that when these two met as respective leaders in Australia in 1960–1, conditions were ideal for a happy series. However, because the West Indies were being written down before they arrived, it took some time before it became apparent that this was going to be an outstanding tour. Then it went with a bang. The two captains and their teams kept cricket supporters in a continual state of excitement which culminated in Benaud leading Australia to victory in the most pulsating series since the war. Both skippers deserve equal credit for the way they revitalized the game. It was the highlight of Benaud's career and everything that came afterwards, including a somewhat uninspiring trip by the M.C.C. under Ted Dexter in 1963, was something of an anticlimax.

As is common these days, especially for Australians, Richie Benaud retired from international cricket while he was still a top-class player. He has resumed work as a journalist and, as one would expect, is proving an exceptional cricket correspondent, although, like many Australians, he is (or certainly was) perhaps hypersensitive about throwing. In addition to his press work, he has become an excellent commentator on both radio and T.V. and is rated highly by the hardest of critics, the active cricketers themselves. I always find his comments objective and full of interest.

Was it the menace and the subtlety of his bowling that I remember particularly about Benaud's cricket? Was it the flamboyant power of his driving with the gay flourish after he had completed his stroke? Was it his perpetual menace in the field, especially when standing dangerously close to the bat? Or was it his general efficiency combined with occasional inspired flashes as a captain? Strangely enough it is none of these things – for what I shall never forget is the graceful, almost feline way in which he moved. This made everything he did on the cricket field attractive to watch. He was not only an outstanding all-rounder; he also looked the part.

23

GARFIELD SOBERS

King of the Caribbean

One match which I always recall with particular affection was the final Test against the West Indies in 1954 at Sabina Park. Brian Statham was injured and we believed that our only chance of winning the match was to bat first, put together a large total and hope that our three spinners – Laker, Wardle and Lock – would be able to winkle out the opposition. We lost the toss on a beautiful track which was bare and glistened in the hot sun, but nevertheless managed to remove the opposition for 139 so that we were batting ourselves by the close of play on the first day. It seemed impossible at the time and in retrospect appears even more so. For my own part, I might, if fate and luck were very kind, conceivably take seven West Indian wickets on a helpful English pitch, but not against that strong batting side out there. However, apart from winning by nine wickets, and the purely personal angle of the best bowling performance of my life, the game was made memorable for me because it was the first time I encountered the man who was to become, in my opinion, the greatest all-rounder the world has seen, Gary Sobers. At the time he was a mere boy and had been selected as an orthodox slow left-hander to replace Alf Valentine who had met with little success in the previous two Tests. Sobers had played against the M.C.C. for Barbados, a match which I missed, which obviously meant that he was an outstanding prospect. However, we had been rather more impressed with his batting than his bowling which, on that pitch, had never looked much better than adequate.

In his first Test for the West Indies Gary went in at number nine, was characteristically not out 14 in their catastrophic first innings and held us up for some time with a useful 26 in the

KING CRICKET

Roy Ullyett.

second. As a slow left-armer he already had a fine control of length and on a wicket as good as that did very well to finish with 4 for 75. Quite plainly, he had come to stay.

Incidentally, I had the distinction, though I did not appreciate it at the time, of being his very first Test victim. I had opened the batting with Len Hutton and we were going along contentedly, but on reaching 43 I attempted an over-ambitious square cut off Gary. The ball bounced a shade more than expected and I was caught at the wicket.

The next time I saw Gary was when he came to England in 1957 under John Goddard with a West Indian side which failed to play to its potential and was soundly thrashed by a powerful England team, losing three of the Tests by an innings and coming close to defeat in the other two. However, Gary showed very plainly that his batting had made an enormous advance and he was already a left-hand bat of power and charm. Although he made a double century against Nottingham, whom now eleven years later he is captaining, his finest innings was 66 in the second Test at Lord's, made out of 261. The pitch was a seam bowler's delight with an uneven bounce and movement off the wicket. In these trying conditions he held out for some four hours, until to my delight he was caught, having edged a delivery from me which left him appreciably. I already knew him to be an exciting striker of the ball and now realized that he also had the ability and the determination to make runs when things were unpleasant. He was plainly destined to become a great batsman, but by comparison his slow left-arm bowling seemed distinctly mundane, a useful relief rather than an incisive destroyer. However, his fielding was certainly exceptional. His reactions were very fast and he was a beautiful mover.

Gary is a glorious batsman to watch and horror to bowl against, because he makes the accumulation of runs seem so inevitable. His defence has a rocklike reliability, his strokes, played with the grandeur of a full swing and follow-through, have the distinctive beauty of all the truly great left-handers, and his judgement of length and line is so good and accurate that he is able to clip a ball away to the boundary off his legs which the average performer would be more than happy to stop. However, his finest characteristic, which I saw for the first time at Lord's that day, is his ability to produce his best in times of stress. In the past there was a tendency to write off the West Indians, sometimes with justification, when the going was hard; they were magnificent in control, but had a tendency to fold when the opposition appeared to have taken command. Under the leadership of Sir Frank Worrell they showed that they had the ability to come back, and now, led and inspired by Gary, they have further emphasized this point. In the second Test match of 1966 England appeared to be in complete control and to have virtually won the match until the arrival of the unique Sobers on the scene. He inspired and nursed his cousin, the comparatively inexperienced Holford, in a wonderful rescue act which has seldom been equalled, but he himself was to surpass even this feat at Sabina Park in the second Test of the 1967–8 M.C.C. tour. His side were following on, the pitch was unreliable in the extreme, and he himself was on a 'king pair'. Not only did he save his side with an undefeated 113, but he made a declaration which in Test match parlance was not only distinctly brave but psychologically brilliant. Despite his long stay at the crease he opened the bowling himself, snatched two wickets (Boycott and Cowdrey) in his first over, and very nearly won a match which everybody believed the West Indians had lost. Gary is one of the greatest retrievers of lost matches and, because his own batting technique is so outstanding, he even has the ability to carry the battle back into the enemy's camp. Never again can it be said that the West Indies are unable to fight back.

The sporting firm, Slazengers, wished to have a West Indian batsman of star calibre to autograph their bats and during Gary's first tour to this country I was asked to make a recommendation. I suggested Sobers, Kanhai and the late Collie Smith. This trio all came from different areas, which suited the export market, and all were exciting players as well as potentially great artists. In other words they possessed exceptional spectator appeal, batting in the way everyone would most like to be able to do.

When the M.C.C. went to the West Indies in 1959–60 they found that Sobers had indeed developed into a batsman of the

highest calibre. In the previous winter he had had a highly successful tour of India and Pakistan. He showed an even greater
partiality for Peter May's attack, scoring 709 runs in the series,
thus breaking the aggregate record which had formerly been held
by George Headley, averaging over a hundred, and failing by
only eight runs to produce a century in every centre. He was
patently the finest left-hander in the world, but he remained
primarily a master batsman who could bowl, rather than an
all-rounder.

Because I played a large amount of international cricket as an
all-rounder, and know from practical experience the problems it
presents, I doubt if anyone can appreciate the worth of Gary
Sobers more. He is, quite simply, the most complete cricketer of
my lifetime and almost certainly in the entire history of the game.
Wally Hammond might have run him close if he had really concentrated on his bowling, but he did not. Wally Hammond was a
tremendous batsman, a magnificent fieldsman, a superb natural
athlete – whatever game he took up he was in a very short time
better than anyone else – and a bowler of international calibre
when he wanted to be, or was roused. However, he never was an
all-rounder in the truest sense of the word and never achieved
the 'double', while Sobers, on the other hand, became the first
man to do the 'double' of 1,000 runs and 50 wickets in a season
of Australian cricket, which is an infinitely more difficult feat.

Gary is a complete batsman, because he has all the strokes, im-
provises splendidly, possesses a remarkable temperament, is invariably entertaining and, once set, makes remarkably few mistakes.
On a good pitch the best chance a bowler has of dismissing him
is to catch him when he is stale because of his efforts with the ball,
in the field and as captain. Alternatively, Gary often takes about
twenty or thirty minutes to become acclimatized and is therefore
slightly vulnerable early on, although once he has reached the
thirties there is an inevitability about another big score. At the
start of an innings he sometimes, like so many left-handers, fishes
outside the off stump. I have bowled against him when he had
played too much cricket and was so physically and mentally tired
that he looked ordinary. It is also true that occasionally he finds

it difficult to concentrate in a minor match, while he is quite obviously at his best on the big occasion. In League cricket his figures have always been impressive, but he could probably have scored even more runs if he really thought them vital. He was content that his team should finish at the top of the table, which was the main objective. However, they still speak in awe of one stroke he played against Wes Hall bowling flat out which sent the ball for a six without any apparent effort.

Gary is also the most complete bowler I have encountered, because he is three distinct bowlers wrapped up in one. He is an orthodox slow left-hander, a wrist spinner and a deadly fast-medium seamer. Other cricketers have been able to vary their styles of bowling to some degree, but nobody has ever been good enough to prove an effective wicket-taker at international level in three different roles. This means that those responsible for selecting any side which contains Gary can afford to carry an extra batsman without weakening its attack.

I rate his slow orthodox left-hand bowling as his least formidable skill. He is accurate, changes his pace well and has, as one would expect, a very useful faster ball, but he is not a big finger-spinner. On the other hand there have been numerous slow left-armers, who although not as good as Gary in this department, have still been chosen to play in Test cricket.

As a bowler of Chinamen and googlies Gary, like all this comparatively rare breed, is apt to prove expensive; but at Test match level this method has three advantages over the orthodox finger-spinner. First, on a plumb wicket, he has the ability to deceive even a great player by the break, whereas in his role as an orthodox slow left-armer he would have to rely more upon tying down the opposition, beating them in the air and hoping for a batting mistake. Secondly, it is one of the best methods of achieving a kill when runs do not matter and the opposition has settled for a draw. Thirdly, it is always liable to bamboozle a 'tail', especially in a stubborn rearguard action. If Gary had decided to concentrate on wrist-spin and bowled nothing else, he would in all probability have become the best in the world, because he certainly spins the ball and has a googly which is not easy to detect.

As it is I would rate him a dangerous bowler in this style, but his control as yet is not perfect enough, nor his armoury large enough (Jack Walsh, the Australian slow left-armer, who played for Leicestershire, had three different googlies) for him to be in the highest class. Personally, I prefer to face Gary when he is bowling in this way, because although I know he may well claim my wicket he will probably provide me with some succulent long-hops and full tosses.

The third string to the Sobers' bowling bow is fast-medium seamer, and though it took him longer to reach the top in this department than in the others it is now his most devastating form of attack. In his early days the West Indies had an abundance of supporting seamers with men like Sir Frank Worrell, Dennis Atkinson and Gerry Gomez, so that there was no cause for him to break into their particular field. It was not until the early 1960s, when Worrell was doing rather less bowling, that Sobers began to show skill as a third seamer. By the mid-1960s he improved so much that in addition to providing Wes Hall and Charlie Griffith with great support he became a quick bowler in his own right and could do more with the new ball than either of them.

It is interesting that a high percentage of the top-class spinners start out as seamers, but comparatively few seamers have begun their first-class careers as slow bowlers. This has probably proved a considerable advantage to Gary, because it enabled him to avoid the danger of being bowled out in his early days. But how good is he as a fast bowler? At the moment I would rate him as potentially the most dangerous new ball player in the world, not the equal of Alan Davidson in his prime, but certainly in the same category, if not better, than Bill Johnston. His threat with the new ball is the same as Davidson's, the ability to move the ball into a right-hander from over the wicket. His pace, if not truly fast all the time, is decidedly sharp and made all the more menacing by his short easy approach while his quicker ball is very hostile. His action is technically perfect, and is the reason why he is able to generate so much speed with so little apparent effort. In 1967 I was managing the Rothmans World XI which he was captaining in the warm-up match against Sussex at Hove. Gary was understandably tired at the end of another season and said he did not intend to bowl very much in the Sussex second innings. However, he took the new ball, slipped into his effortless groove and bowled superbly for an hour and a half. It seemed to me and the batsmen that he was even faster and more menacing at the end than at the beginning of the spell!

Nobody can consider himself a genuine all-rounder unless he is good in the field. Gary more than fulfils this qualification : he is a superb all-round fieldsman, a brilliant outfielder, a wonderful catcher close to the bat, especially at backward short leg, or in the slips where he is of the highest class. I have never seen him keep wicket, but I am sure he would have little difficulty in excelling behind the stumps if that were his desire!

Although I knew and respected Gary Sobers as a cricketer it was not until he came to England on a short trip with a West Indian side under Sir Frank Worrell that I really began to know him as a person. This was the year following their triumphant visit here in 1963 and it was my happy, interesting and easy job to look after them. Living with them gave me a new concept of West Indians. I began to understand them so much better and like them so much more. I gained the impression that in the past there had been a tendency for them to regard me with some suspicion, while I suppose I had never thought objectively enough about them. My association with Gary himself continued in the next few years. I managed the World side of which he was inevitably a member and was eventually to lead with so much verve and distinction. I captained the International Cavaliers on a trip to Jamaica and Barbados which was sponsored by Carreras, and Gary played against us in both islands. He is of course the uncrowned king of Barbados and he took me to parts of that lovely little island to which the ordinary tourist never goes. In addition I played with him, under him and against him for the Cavaliers in numerous enjoyable Sunday afternoon matches. The more often I saw him play the greater he appeared.

But Gary is also, of course, a hard and ruthless cricketer. This is inevitable when you consider his background. Although Barbados is a delightful island, it is also small, over-crowded, and the chances of advancement and acquiring wealth distinctly limited. Gary himself was brought up in a neighbourhood where there was never enough money available for luxuries, indeed not enough for what we in this country now consider necessities. This did not mean that he was unhappy, but life was inevitably something of a struggle, with too many people competing for too few jobs. Because of his ability to play cricket superbly, Gary was able to conquer these difficulties, but without determination as well as skill it is unlikely he would have succeeded. Runs to Gary not only brought pleasure, they enabled him to raise his standard of living. He may play like a cavalier, but behind the gaiety is a steely purposefulness to win. The public are inclined to believe that all West Indian cricketers are like those carefree calypsos they sing so well, Calypso kids, but in fact they can be as stubborn and as obdurate as a Yorkshireman. Even if this is not their nature, Sobers certainly leads a team with the same dedication and it is not without significance that Barbados is looked upon in the Caribbean rather in the same way as Yorkshire in this country. Tactically he is sound and quite a canny captain who with years ahead of him may well become even more outstanding, while his own performances in every facet of the game serve as a wonderful inspiration to any team. He is a remarkably unselfish cricketer and has always been prepared to sacrifice personal glory in the interests of his side, although on occasions one feels he has batted himself too low in the order. This unselfishness has become even more important since he was given the captaincy of the West Indies. He knows that it pays to attack, but there are many occasions when defence either in the field or with the bat is tactically more likely to bring about the desired result, the destruction or, on occasions, merely the frustration of the enemy. However, he is also by inclination a gambler while his own superiority is sometimes responsible for his underrating the opposition. Certainly no Yorkshireman would have been as generous as when he declared for the second time against England at Trinidad in 1968. Although he set a high run rate in terms of Test cricket, he did this without possessing a break in the shape of fast bowlers with long runs. It seems to me that he was thinking more in terms of

runs per hour than the vital one of runs per over. England
certainly chased the target intelligently and well, but their players
have plenty of experience in doing just this in county cricket. It
could be argued in defence of Sobers that this was his only chance
of winning the match, while his declaration undoubtedly transformed a dull draw into an exciting finish, provided fine entertainment for the spectators and was one of the most sporting ever
to be made in Test cricket, especially when one remembers that
the West Indies had outplayed Cowdrey's feats throughout this
particular contest. Declarations of this nature are rare, almost
unique in international matches, because each is only part of the
complete whole which goes to make up the series. If Gary had
acted in this fashion when a win was the only possible way he
could have gained the rubber, nobody could have complained,
although in those circumstances I have my doubts as to whether
England would have accepted the bait. What was odd about his
action was not that the West Indies lost, but that the chances of
winning were so heavily stacked against him. He gave England
the opportunity to carry off the campaign, which they did and
certainly deserved, without ever being in serious danger of defeat,
bearing in mind the time available and the condition of the wicket.
Although Cowdrey's men had collapsed dramatically at Sabina
Park, the pitch had then been very untrustworthy and there was
never any real hope of their scoring the runs because Gary was
always in the position of being able to shut the game up by employing his pacemen. It might also be said that if his decision was
not made on the spur of the moment without considering all the
various factors involved, why did not his own side attack the bowling with much more abandon in their own second innings? Therefore I must inevitably come to the conclusion that this declaration,
though gallant and stimulating, must also be considered, both at
the time and in retrospect, tactically foolhardy. It could mark the
beginning of charitable Test cricket, but I do not really believe it.
I have never had much sympathy with those who support the
idea that the game is the thing and the result does not matter.
Winning must always be the first consideration and then, when
this becomes impossible or unlikely because of the other side hold-

ing all the trumps, one must do one's utmost to secure a draw. This is surely the only way to approach international sport.

Gary possesses a keen sense of fun, approaches life with gaiety and loves to laugh loud and often. He has a splendid disregard for the morrow which is sometimes the despair of his advisers, as he is a natural spender. Why worry about *mañana* when today is bubbling? He has been endowed with such a splendid physique, exceptional stamina and ability, that he has had no difficulty in maintaining his position as a world class athlete without having to worry overmuch about training. He once joined a Commonwealth side in India after a long flight from Australia. Although he had had no sleep it made no difference to his performance on the field where he bowled like an angel and batted like a god. He is one of that very small select group of players who is just as likely to make a century, or cause a collapse with the ball, when he has not been to bed, as if he had retired at ten-thirty. He loves racing, is prepared to have a bet on most things, and enjoys food, drink and good fellowship. He makes golf appear a comparatively simple game and it is difficult to believe that he would have been other than outstanding at any sport he chose to take up. Impulsive and generous, he makes an interesting and sometimes, because of his vitality, a somewhat exhausting companion.

The record books are packed with his exploits and it is difficult to single out instances of his mastery of cricket because they are so many. However, two minor examples I shall never forget occurred in Sunday Cavalier matches. The first was at Hove on a wet, sodden pitch. Tony Buss of Sussex bowled a good-length leg-cutter which bit, turned and stood up. It was a near-perfect delivery which would have accounted for many players and anyone would have been satisfied to stop, but Gary went majestically on to his back foot and battered it with a straight bat. His timing was so perfect that he was able to send it along the ground to the boundary without anyone having time to move, despite the fact that the outfield was sluggish and fours practically non-existent. On the second occasion I was bowling in my Testimonial Match; there were wickets in hand and the allotted span of overs almost used up. I bowled what I considered a highly satisfactory ball which pitched around the off stump and hit the middle. Both the wicket-keeper and first slip came up and congratulated me, because they did not realize that Gary Sobers had deliberately presented me with his wicket. Anyone can chuck his wicket away, but only an artist can do it so convincingly that even the wicket-keeper and first slip are deceived!

24

THE BARNACLE

Publisher's Note: At this stage, it struck us that this book, as a picture of a whole period of cricket, lacked a portrait of the author, himself one of the major figures of that period. We have therefore persuaded him, despite his protests, to trace his own experiences and development and to analyse his character and technique as a cricketer.

Cricket has been one of the main interests in my life from the age of three. In those pre-school days most of it was played in my back garden and on the beach where my parents used to have a tent or, to be more accurate, on the mud at Westcliff. There were occasions when I was unable to find anyone else who shared my passion for the game, which was hardly surprising as six-thirty on a summer morning was my ideal time to start. This led me to invent my own version which consisted of bowling against the back of the house and hitting the return with a small stump; I was both bowler and batsman and this may unconsciously have been the reason for my eventually becoming an all-rounder. For that matter, both on the beach and in the garden, it was essential to be able to bat and bowl as often there were only two performers and, even when the numbers increased, it was clearly profitable to be able to do both.

As there were no umpires in my early cricket nobody worried that I threw rather than bowled. I had been endowed with a strong, powerful arm and, like most small boys, I wanted to be a fast bowler. Harold Larwood was my hero. When I was given the Jack Hobbs account of the 'Bodyline' tour as a Christmas present I immediately transformed a very muddy garden in Westcliff from White Hart Lane into the Melbourne Oval so that I could

stage my own imaginary fight for the Ashes, where England naturally triumphed.

My career as a thrower (which might have passed unnoticed in the early 1960s) continued until one day on the beach our 'pick up' game was invaded by a number of adults who did not appreciate the spade wickets being knocked out by some fierce chucking with a wet tennis ball. My father told me that I would either have to bowl under-arm or throw more slowly. This was a serious blow to a would-be Larwood but one morning my brother showed me how to bowl legitimately and in a pleasantly short period I found that I was able to propel a ball fairly, accurately and quite quickly – which more than upholds my contention that bowling is ninety per cent aptitude combined with a willingness to practise.

At the age of eight I was sent to Alleyn Court Preparatory School and was fortunate that my arrival coincided with the late Denys Wilcox, who was captain of Cambridge University and later of Essex, succeeding his father as headmaster. He was fanatically keen on games, especially cricket, and was also a fine coach. Until that time I had relied on a good eye, but he patiently showed me that there was very much more to making runs. The very first time he had me in a net provided both a salutary lesson and positive proof of this, because I found I could not consistently hit good length under-arm deliveries – which I regarded with some scorn – consistently out of the net. He made me realize that it paid to play straight. In my final summer at Alleyn Court I scored over 1,100 runs in eleven matches with a top score of 200 and a lowest of 50, and in addition captured some 50 wickets. Obviously I was never again able to dominate the game to such a degree and in the light of later events it is interesting to note what Denys Wilcox wrote:

His batting and fielding reached as high a standard as anyone could expect of a preparatory schoolboy. There are immense possibilities about his bowling, too, but perhaps it will be wise for him to concentrate on his batting in the future. All-rounders are invaluable, but one often sees a young cricketer who is a good batsman and a good bowler but never reaches the highest class at either.

In county cricket today there are very few players who are first class with the bat and the ball. There is so much more cricket played now that it requires a man of exceptional stamina to do both. It is noticeable that when an all-rounder is in exceptional form with the ball his batting suffers, and vice versa.

Although I knew that Denys was correct I obstinately decided that I would be an exception to the general rule. When I arrived at Dulwich College the First XI happened to be an exceptionally powerful school side and there seemed no likelihood of my making the team until Jack Robertson, in scoring a beautiful century for a M.C.C. XI, underlined certain deficiencies in the attack. The outcome was that I was picked at fourteen as the opening fast bowler : the biggest thrill of my entire career was when Alan Shirreff, the captain, told me that I was in the side to play against Bedford on Saturday. For the rest of that week I was in a perpetual dream and had to leave the classroom more frequently than usual to check that it really was my name on the list pinned up outside the main hall.

C. S. 'Father' Marriott was in charge of cricket at Dulwich and he was another who felt, after my first year, that my future lay as a batsman. He also fancied that I might develop into a slow leg-break bowler and one season, handicapped by a bad back which prevented me bowling quickly, I experimented with this form of attack. However, in one match, having taken one wicket – with my quicker ball – for plenty, I reverted to pace. I then and there thrust aside any idea of being anything else but a batsman *and* quick bowler. I would have made more runs or taken more wickets if I had decided to concentrate on one or the other, but this is one decision I have never regretted. I could never have enjoyed the game so much and I also believe that I would have retired sooner. In the twilight of my career in county cricket I still gained satisfaction from comparatively small scores with the bat and odd wickets, and did not become as bored with six-day cricket as might have happened if I had had only one string to my bow.

The all-rounder has a considerable psychological advantage over the specialist with bat or ball, because there is the comforting knowledge that if he fails at one he has the opportunity to rectify matters with the other. This ensured that I was never nervous bowling and considerably less nervous when going in to bat than most players. The chief problem was the physical difficulty of playing six and often seven days per week. This was made harder in my case because Essex were often short of runs and always short of bowling power. In school and club cricket there is no problem in combining batting and bowling but it can be a strain in English first class cricket. That is why there is such a shortage of genuine all-rounders.

A long innings, I found, was always liable to take the edge off my bowling, while I found it very difficult to bat if I had just come off the field after bowling thirty overs, because my feet simply would not move fast enough. As I have never minded where I batted there was much to be said for my going in early when we batted first and down the order when we had just spent a long day in the field, but this did not take into account that batsmen have a habit of becoming possessive and jealous about their position in a batting line-up. Not only are they liable to resent a change, but are only too ready to use it as a built-in excuse in case of failure. For Essex I batted mainly at numbers five and six, which meant that I ran out of partners rather too often and acquired a remarkable number of 'stars'. Although I was frequently pressed into service as an opener for England, I was never sufficiently qualified, nor did I carry enough fire power, and unquestionably I was better suited to the middle of the order.

From Dulwich I went straight into the Royal Marines, but I was fortunate to play a considerable amount of cricket, including matches for the Royal Navy and the British Empire XI. Although I regarded myself as an all-rounder, I was employed mainly as a fast bowler who could bat, a view which was enhanced by my claiming three wickets in my first over in a four counties match at Lord's. However, when I made my début for Essex against Derbyshire after the war I was asked to open the batting and the bowling and from that time I was always chosen as an all-rounder except on the odd occasions when I was injured.

In those early days for Essex and for Cambridge University (1946-8) I was a lively, somewhat unpredictable bowler who hurled the ball down as quickly as possible. Rather surprisingly in view of later developments, I was also considered a reasonably fast-scoring bat who liked to drive and was decidedly tucked up on my legs. I once even managed to score a double century in well under a day against a not particularly venomous Sussex attack!

1948 was to prove a decisive year. First, I married. Second, I came down from Cambridge and became Assistant Secretary to Essex C.C.C., instead of joining the teaching profession which had been my original intention. Third, although it was a very bad season from the cricket angle, I learned a great deal. Earlier I had declined to be considered for the West Indian tour under G. O. Allen, and then the Australians arrived in England and bulldozed their way through the counties. They made me realize that I was not nearly as good as I'd hoped. For one thing, facing Lindwall and Miller convinced me that there was not the slightest chance of my ever becoming a second Larwood and that therefore I would have to develop into an accurate seamer if I was going to progress much further. During the ensuing winter I cut out one of the whirls in my action, which gave me greater rhythm and control, and was very gratified to find myself selected for England in the following season against the New Zealanders as an opening bowler. I was not genuinely quick, but sufficiently lively to produce a bouncer that had a reasonable chance of scoring a direct hit on a batsman. However, there was still a long way to go, as in the following summer my action was not sufficiently grooved to prevent me losing my run-up in a Test Match against the West Indies – a horrible experience, this. However, the control was steadily improving so that by the time I went to Australia with the M.C.C. in 1950-1 I felt I could hold my own in the best company. I had also begun to think seriously about the game with a view to making the best possible use of what I could do as both a batsman and a bowler. I worked out the most effective way for me to bowl against each player and how to use the fieldsmen whether pressing home an advantage or attempting to keep the opposition quiet. I learned that it often paid to attack a batsman through his strength as well as the more obvious way of through his weakness. In other words if an Australian batsman was especially strong off his legs I would often bowl at his leg stump and reinforce the on side, because he would probably milk me out there, once well settled, even when I attacked his off stump. Neil Harvey, if one can say a great player is ever vulnerable, was a shade suspect outside the off stump early on, while Keith Miller plainly hated to be tied down.

The next important date in my cricket career was 1953 when we regained the Ashes. In this series I gained the dubious distinction of being generally regarded as a defensive batsman, because, as my statistician friends informed me, I batted far longer than anyone else. I was labelled the 'Barnacle' and in time people began to expect me to bat with extreme caution and stay a long time. In Australia I had only to emerge from the pavilion to be greeted with ' 'ave a go, Bailey, yer mug' which was liable to become considerably more colourful if I was inconsiderate enough to occupy the crease for a lengthy spell. The English batting line-up of those days had a long 'tail' and it became accepted that my role was to seal up one end until the arrival of number eleven. This suited me, as I enjoyed batting more when the pressure was on; after all, this was no new experience as Essex had always shown a marked tendency to collapse. It was eventually said, with some justification, that if a crisis did not occur I would manufacture one. Having found myself cast in the role of stubborn stone-waller, I eventually began to believe in it myself. It rather appealed to my sense of humour and certainly never worried me. Providing I thought I was doing the right thing for my side by plodding slowly along I gained a perverse satisfaction from it. Some players are liable to be affected by a hostile reaction from the crowd, but if anything a slow handclap only made me the more obdurate and more determined not to fail. It always seemed a dreadful waste to struggle for hours for relatively few runs and then lose one's wicket through a piece of carelessness. What did I think about while in the middle? Quite simply not getting out.

The biggest problem about playing a protracted innings occurred for me after the crisis had been negotiated and when it was desirable to increase the tempo of scoring. If I had been batting for a couple of hours with not getting out my primary concern, I found the utmost difficulty in switching, if not to gay abandon, at least to attack, because by that time I had become attuned to regarding every delivery as full of menace. When I went in to bat for England with the score at 100 for 4 my intention was simple, not to lose my wicket and to get off the mark. Once these two objectives had been attained I would aim for double figures, and from that moment – a superstitious quirk – I would not look at the scoreboard until the fall of the next wicket. My aims were never grandiose, just another ten runs and then start again. The big disadvantage of making survival the main consideration is that one automatically misses many opportunities to score. One is so busy thinking in terms of keeping the bowlers out that one tends to be surprised by the loose ball.

In time I became so accustomed to my role that I often unconsciously embellished it until it almost became part of myself. Although my stroke repertoire had never been extensive, it had been adequate enough aided by singles, which I have always sought, and edges, which I have never despised, to keep the runs coming at a respectable pace; but the more I became known as the 'Barnacle' the more restricted I tended to become and the earlier I committed myself to the front foot. On those occasions when quick runs were wanted I would try to think in terms of scoring boundaries which sometimes led me into that usually fatal act of pre-selection, and occasionally I would allow myself a flippant innings, but it was as out of character as a 'heavy' appearing in musical comedy.

Looking back I sometimes wonder to what extent circumstances, and Test cricket in particular, were responsible for my becoming a stone-waller. Would I have been an entirely different player if I had been brought up in Kent where the pitches were normally good and encouraged stroke-making, or was there always an inclination towards the passive which had been merely subdued in my early days? I cannot really say, but I do remember

P. G. Wodehouse coming down to Dulwich to watch a match against St Paul's and writing an account for the magazine. I was at the crease for some time on that occasion without contributing many runs. P. G. Wodehouse summed things up beautifully: 'Bailey awoke from an apparent coma to strike a boundary.' So perhaps it was always lurking beneath the surface and just needed the situation to bring it out; but neither did I forget the words of Denys Wilcox, 'stay there and the runs are bound to come'.

It has been said that nobody likes playing really fast bowling, but some show it rather more than others. However, I always relished a battle against pace. The element of physical danger added spice to the situation, while it was also easier to keep the scoreboard ticking over when the speed of the ball did so much of the work for the batsman. In truth I was short of imagination in this particular respect and never imagined, often quite incorrectly, that I would be hit, while I also gained particular satisfaction from frustrating the aims of the fast bowlers. As a breed they are easily riled. Even more important these tactics paid because, once they had lost their temper, they were inclined to think more about knocking my head off than bowling me out.

Facing pace on a lively pitch made the game especially interesting. In one match against Derbyshire, Essex had spent the majority of the day in the pavilion playing cards, when suddenly and unexpectedly we had to sally forth for the final two hours to face a fresh Les Jackson and Harold Rhodes in dubious light. The ball kept lifting off a full length and batting proved a hazardous business with each delivery posing a new problem. Doug Insole and I did not score many runs that night, but the hour together before the welcome final over was one of our most satisfying partnerships.

Because of my pronounced initial forward movement it followed that I played a high percentage of fast bowling with my weight on my front foot. This meant I could never hook effectively as I did not have sufficient time to move into the correct position. It also necessitated me learning how to 'give' at the moment of contact when a ball suddenly lifts. This is an especially important technique on the untrustworthy pitch since it enables one to 'drop' the ball dead even when struck on the gloves. Very occasionally against someone like Frank Tyson or Neil Adcock on a fast pitch I have moved back initially. I also found it paid to do this against pace on a really bad wicket when the ball was liable to rear off a length. In these circumstances to thrust forward was inevitably disastrous, but on the back foot there was a chance.

Another especially satisfying time to bat is on a 'sticky' against two good spinners, when the ball is lifting and turning. To exist in these conditions one needs ingenuity, a sound technique, and a certain amount of luck, especially at the start. There have been many occasions when I have gone in to bat and could not see the slightest likelihood of my staying, but if I was fortunate enough to negotiate the first three overs it became progressively more feasible. On a 'sticky' while it is necessary to 'give' with the ball on impact even when employing the deadest of dead bats, also it frequently pays to take a calculated risk with an attacking shot from time to time, especially when the opposition tend to crowd close and there are vacant areas in the outfield. In these circumstances, with the length of one's survival somewhat limited, I was always more prepared to play a lofted shot than on a good wicket, when the slight risk involved was seldom justified. Thirty runs made on a bad wicket has always given me infinitely more pleasure and satisfaction than a hundred on a plumb track, even though the latter will be listed in the records books. Perhaps, because I have always been an all-rounder, records have meant less to me than most. Some cricketers can tell you the exact number of runs they have scored in any of their important innings, and have an exact knowledge of every knock in the current season. I have frequently come in from batting without knowing my total until I read it in the paper on the following day, while on one occasion I completed the 'double' and did not realize it until it was pointed out.

Looking back over twenty years one question springs to mind, was it all worth while? The answer is an unequivocal yes. I gained more satisfaction from playing first class cricket than would be possible from any other team game. I loved soccer and in fact looked forward far more to the match on Saturday after-noon than to a cricket match, because it was a much rarer event. Throughout the summer cricket occupied six, and often seven days a week, quite apart from overseas tours. The fact that one can still enjoy a sport that is so time-consuming is in itself remarkable. The reason lies in cricket being essentially a game of ebb and flow with a charm which comes from the situation. The extent and the variety of the situations which arise are so endless that despite playing so much I was never satiated. There were occasions when I became bored (and tired mentally), but these were rare. I al-ways found that knocking someone's stump out of the ground, or hitting a boundary never failed to excite, while it was not pos-sible to be anything but thrilled when the side wanted ten to win and our last pair were together. In between lethargic spells cricket does produce a tension which can become almost unbearable. I always found the most nerve-wracking moments occurred when I personally was helpless, as in a Gillette cup match against Derby after I had been run out by my runner at a time when we appeared to be cruising to a comfortable win. In a matter of mo-ments the whole course of the match changed for the worse, and all I could do was hope and curse. When I was in the field or batting, the more I was personally involved at vital stages the more enjoyable it all became. To hit the winning run with nine wickets down, to take the final wicket in the last over with two runs re-quired, or to frustrate the enemy by forcing a draw when victory was no longer possible were to me moments of unadulterated pleasure. In later years as captain, when the success of the team meant more, and personal success had less attraction, I gained enormous satisfaction from the deeds of players like Barry Knight, Keith Fletcher, and Brian Taylor, whom I had signed on straight from school so many years before.

In one respect I was luckier than most players. Besides playing the game, as Assistant Secretary and later Secretary of Essex I was also involved in its administration. Although this had certain disadvantages (such as settling down to deal with some well over-due correspondence on the ground and suddenly finding it neces-sary to rush frantically to the pavilion because there had been a collapse) it gave me yet another interest in cricket. Sometimes I think, indeed, that perhaps my most important contribution to the game was being an original member of the Gillette Cup Committee. Unlike so many cricket committees this was small and well balanced. The rules and regulations which we first drew up have hardly been altered and the competition turned out to be an even bigger success than we imagined.

I was asked once if I felt that I had reached the standards I hoped and I was able to say truthfully that I had achieved far more than I expected. When I decided to play first class cricket regularly in 1948, I hoped that I might eventually be picked for England, but never for one moment did I imagine myself as a regular. If I had known, I would certainly have turned professional as this would have proved so much more remunerative. What, on the other hand, has always been a mystery to me is why so many players of greater ability have not done better.

Obviously I have had disappointments. I was written off as an international in 1959 after I returned from Australia for the third and least successful time. I had been handicapped throughout this time by back trouble which did not clear up until it was successfully manipulated in the following summer. The outcome was that, though I was never chosen for further Tests I was batting and bowling better than I had ever done. For one thing my image no longer fitted. Nevertheless, I had played in far more internationals than I had ever envisaged.

The one thing which I really would have liked to have done was to lead Essex to victory in the County Championship, but, to be honest, we needed an enormous amount of luck to make up for the playing deficiencies. Again, it would have been pleasant to captain England, especially abroad, but I had foreseen that those responsible for making the appointment would not consider me suitable, and was not upset when I was not selected.

For cricket has been generous to me. It has enabled me to visit, under the best possible circumstances, places which would otherwise have remained for me exotic names on a map. The hospitality I have encountered has been magnificent. I have been thoroughly spoilt and I enjoyed it. My one regret now is that I have never thanked my many hosts enough. In company with many English cricketers I tended to expect the special treatment received as a right rather than as a privilege and became blasé. Alas, players seldom appreciate how lucky they are at the time.

I believed, until very recently, that County cricket six days per week would continue to exist for the foreseeable future. But cricket is now having to struggle with new competitors and it is not helped by well-meaning experts who try to improve it by new legislation which nearly always fails to solve anything. Essex once put a resolution to the Advisory County Cricket Committee to the effect that there should be no changes to the Rules for three years. Everyone seemed to agree that this was desirable, especially the players, but it was not accepted. These constant changes have in the long run proved a handicap to the game.

Again, the financial returns to players have failed to keep step with the cost of living, so that as a career County cricket is no longer quite as attractive as it used to be for the ordinary performer. Cricket cannot now command, outside of the Tests and certain key matches, the types of gates to make it an even vaguely sound commercial proposition. Without Supporters Associations, football pools and various extraneous methods of raising money a number of the county clubs would have already ceased to exist. One of the solutions to these economic difficulties lies in an increasing use of commercial sponsorship and at last this is being appreciated. Firms of all kinds and sizes are now being encouraged to assist the sport in practical ways, which range from providing lunch to bringing a World Eleven to England.

There had always been financial problems, but now it has become clear that County cricket in its existing form will have to change because of the shortage of money and spectators. The clubs have just started to realize that Sunday has the largest crowd potential and 1969 will see the commencement of a Sunday League of one-day fixtures and a reduction in the number of three-day matches. The counties have been impressed by the success of the Sunday games played by the International Cavaliers (sponsored by Rothmans) and hope that the new competition will prove equally as popular. Sunday cricket has come to stay, but I have doubts as to the wisdom of playing a one-day contest in the middle of a three-day match. This must reduce the continuity and some of the attraction of the longer game. There is also the danger that the quicker tempo of limited-over one-day affairs will have an adverse effect, at least initially, on the more subtle and protracted engagements. No cricketer who has played regular first class cricket can hope to find as much enjoyment and satisfaction in a shortened version with its many artificial restrictions. It simply cannot compare. In addition it must also be remembered that the highest form of cricket, the most publicized, and the best supported are the Test Matches which last five days. The ideal preparation for these is undoubtedly the two-innings game with its ever changing and sometimes leisurely patterns and not the hectic scramble which is both the strength and weakness of the one-day contest.

Looking back, I have no regrets at having devoted such a large portion of my life to cricket. If I could play in the same era I would want to do it all over again. If I had been born ten years later, however, I am not quite so sure.